The Timeless Ten

Ancient Wisdom For Today's World.

Explore the enduring impact of the Ten Commandments, highlighted through Yeshua's teachings, and reveal their wisdom as guides for ethical conduct and spiritual understanding in the modern world.

Terry Brown

"For Susan, my life's companion and soul mate, the heartbeat of my existence for over fifty years. Together, we have walked hand in hand, shared every step, challenge, and triumph, and traversed a journey rich in joy, sorrow, and dreams with unwavering love and support. You have been my compass and confidante, guiding and enriching every moment of our journey together. This book is dedicated to you, with all my love and gratitude for the decades we have shared and the memories we have created."

© All rights reserved. No part of this book may be reproduced or distributed in any form without prior permission from the author except for non-commercial uses permitted by copyright law.

Chapter 1.	Eternal Echoes: Navigating the Intersection of Ancient Wisdom and Contemporary Ethics	**8**
Chapter 2.	Moral Foundations and Modern Societies: The Enduring Influence of the Ten Commandments.	**14**
Chapter 3.	The Heart of the Commandments: Yeshua's Approach to living beyond the letter.	**17**
Chapter 4.	The First Commandment: The Foundation of Faith.	**21**
Chapter 5.	The Second Commandment: Idolatry in the modern age.	**32**
Chapter 6.	The Third Commandment: The power of words.	**44**
Chapter 7.	The Fourth Commandment: A day apart.	**54**
Chapter 8.	The Fifth Commandment: The foundations of respect.	**62**
Chapter 9.	The Sixth Commandment: The Sanctity of Life.	**71**

Chapter 10.	The Seventh Commandment: Fidelity and Trust.	**81**
Chapter 11.	The Eighth Commandment: Integrity in Possessions	**92**
Chapter 12.	The Ninth Commandment: A community of justice and honesty.	**102**
Chapter 13.	The Tenth Commandment: Understanding the value of what we have.	**114**
Chapter 14.	The Wisdom of Yeshua: How Our Inner World Shapes Our Outer Actions.	**125**
Chapter 15.	A Compassionate Shift: The Impact of Living by the Ten Commandments Today, Yeshua's Way.	**143**
Chapter 16.	From Stone Tablets to Modern Hearts: Integrating the Commandments into Daily Life.	**154**
Chapter 17.	In the Company of the Faithful: Accountability as a Pathway and Foundation for Godly Humility.	**156**
Chapter 18.	Yeshua's Teachings: A Self-Reflection	**161**

Chapter 1.

Introduction

Eternal Echoes: Navigating the Intersection of Ancient Wisdom and Contemporary Ethics

Try to imagine a book about the Timeless Ten who decide to join the party where the Famous Five are off on an adventure, the Magnificent Seven are saddling up, and Ocean's Eleven are plotting their next heist.

However, unlike those stories, this book isn't about thrilling escapades or daring missions; it's more about laying down the law - literally. While the others might take you on a rollercoaster ride of suspense and action, the Timeless Ten is here to remind you to call your Mother, not to covet your neighbour's donkey, and generally how to be a good person living an honest and moral lifestyle. It must sound quite dull in comparison.

But if you're looking for a guide on ethical living rather than a blueprint for an elaborate casino robbery, you've picked the right book.

Not so long ago, most individuals could effortlessly recite the Ten Commandments by heart. They adorned the walls of numerous schools and were a staple of Sunday School lessons in local churches, imparting moral guidance to children each week. However, today, it's a different story.

Nowadays, very few people can quote them, and even fewer can arrange them in their correct sequence. Just to mention the Ten Commandments today triggers a mixed bag of responses.

To some, they remain a pivotal moral compass, a timeless guide that lays the groundwork for ethical conduct and principles. For others, they are seen as relics of the past - intriguing maybe, but no longer applicable or pertinent to the complexities of contemporary life.

Regardless of where you stand, there's no denying the profound impact these ancient laws have had on culture, law, and individual lives throughout history.

The Ten Commandments, also known as the Decalogue or the Ten Words, are biblical principles relating to ethics and worship. These rules form the basis of moral codes and legal ethics for millions of people around the world.

Found in the books of Exodus and Deuteronomy, the Commandments were given to Moses by God on Mount Sinai and have since been a central pillar in both religious and secular discussions about morality.

This introduction aims to explore the Ten Commandments in a manner accessible and engaging to everyone, regardless of their background or beliefs. We'll look at the history, significance, and modern interpretations of these ancient directives, shedding light on why they remain a topic of discussion and reverence today.

We will also delve into the teachings and practices of Yeshua (Jesus) as he embodied and communicated them throughout his ministry on earth, offering insights into his perspectives and guidance on these matters.

The story begins with Moses on Mount Sinai, where he received two stone tablets inscribed by God with the Ten Commandments. This momentous event is celebrated and remembered in various religions, particularly Judaism and Christianity, each adding its perspectives and teachings about the Commandments.

Historically, these laws were revolutionary. They provided a moral framework that emphasised the relationship between humans and God and between each other. Concepts like honouring one's parents, refraining from murder, theft, and bearing false witness were foundational in developing a just society.

The Ten Commandments are:

1. *I am the LORD your God, who brought you out from the land of Egypt, where you were slaves.*

2. *You shall have no other gods beside me. You shall not make any carved image for yourself or a likeness of anything in heaven above, on the earth below, or in the waters under the earth. Do not bow down to them or be subservient to them, for I, the LORD your God, am a jealous God. I follow up on the guilt of the fathers with their children, their grandchildren, and their great-grandchildren if they also hate me. But I show mercy to thousands who love me and keep my commandments.*

3. *You shall not misuse the name of the LORD your God, for the LORD will not permit anyone who misuses his name to escape unpunished.*

4. *Remember the Sabbath day by setting it apart as holy. Six days, you are to serve and do all your regular work, but the seventh day shall be a sabbath rest to the LORD your God. Do not do any regular work, neither you, nor your sons or daughters, nor your male or female servants, nor your cattle, nor the alien who is residing inside your gates, for in six days the LORD made the heavens and the earth, the sea, and everything that is in them, but he rested on the seventh day. In this way, the LORD blessed the seventh day and made it holy.*

5. *Honour your father and your mother so that you may spend many days on the land that the* Lord *your God is giving to you.*

6. *You shall not commit murder.*

7. *You shall not commit adultery.*

8. *You shall not steal.*

9. *You shall not give false testimony against your neighbour.*

10. *You shall not covet your neighbour's house. You shall not covet your neighbour's wife, male servant, female servant, ox, donkey, or anything else that belongs to your neighbour.*

Exodus 20:2-17

Each Commandment serves a specific purpose in guiding individuals toward ethical behaviour. The first four commandments focus on one's relationship with God, emphasising respect, reverence, and dedication.

The remaining six commandments address interpersonal relationships, advocating for respect, honesty, and fairness in dealing with others.

The Ten Commandments might seem like relics of a bygone era in today's fast-paced, complex world. Yet, their core principles continue to resonate across cultures and societies. They've influenced laws, ethics, and moral philosophies around the globe, underscoring the importance of fairness, respect, and integrity in human interactions.

Many debates and discussions about morality, ethics, and law still reference the Ten Commandments, highlighting their enduring impact. They're seen as religious directives and universal principles that can guide ethical behaviour and decision-making in various contexts.

Interpreting the Ten Commandments in the modern context can be challenging. Society has evolved, and our understanding of morality and ethics has changed. Issues like digital privacy, environmental stewardship, and global human rights are pressing concerns today that weren't explicitly addressed in the ancient texts.

This has led to diverse interpretations and applications of the Commandments. Some view them as immutable laws, while others see them as a starting point for a broader ethical discourse that adapts to changing societal norms and values.

The Ten Commandments have also permeated cultural and educational spheres, influencing art, literature, and public discourse. They serve as a reference point for discussions about moral education, the role of religion in public life, and the intersection of law and ethics.

In many ways, the Ten Commandments have transcended their original religious context to become symbols of universal moral principles. They challenge individuals and societies to reflect on the values that underpin a just and compassionate world.

The Ten Commandments are a testament to the enduring quest for moral guidance and ethical behaviour. As we navigate the complexities of modern life, they offer a foundation upon which to build a framework of values that promote respect, justice, and integrity.

This book aims to explore each commandment in depth, examining its historical context, moral significance, and relevance today, as well as how Yeshua approached it. Whether deeply religious, a secular thinker, or somewhere in between, the journey through the

Ten Commandments is a journey through the heart of human ethics and morality - a reflection on what it means to live a good life.

Understanding these ancient laws allows us to appreciate their wisdom and consider their place in our lives today. The Ten Commandments are not just a list of do's and don'ts; they are a source of inspiration, offering insights into navigating life's challenges with compassion, integrity, and respect for others.

Chapter 2.

Moral Foundations and Modern Societies: The Enduring Influence of the Ten Commandments.

The Ten Commandments, a set of biblical principles relating to ethics and worship, have played a pivotal role in shaping societies' moral and legal frameworks throughout history.

Presented in the book of Exodus and reiterated in Deuteronomy in the Hebrew Bible, these commandments form the bedrock of Judeo-Christian moral teachings. Their influence, however, extends far beyond religious texts and practices, permeating various aspects of modern societies, from legal systems and cultural norms to individual moral decisions.

Originating in a historical context over 3,000 years ago, the Ten Commandments encompassed directives against murder, theft, adultery, and false testimony, as well as the importance of honouring one's parents and observing the Sabbath. These commandments provided a moral code for the Israelites and laid the groundwork for the development of ethical and legal standards worldwide.

The universal appeal of the Ten Commandments can be attributed to their simplicity and the fundamental human values they endorse. These commandments have transcended their religious origins to influence secular moral philosophies and legal principles globally by advocating for respect, honesty, and community well-being.

One of the most significant impacts of the Ten Commandments has been on the development of Western legal systems. Many of the commandments find secular parallels in laws concerning murder, theft, perjury, and protecting family integrity. These parallels are not coincidental; they reflect the profound influence of Judeo-Christian ethical teachings on the formulation of legal codes.

For instance, the prohibition against theft and murder has been universally adopted in legal systems worldwide, underscoring a shared understanding of fundamental rights and wrongs. The emphasis on truth-telling and honouring contracts reflects the commandment against bearing false witness, reinforcing the importance of honesty and trustworthiness in social and economic interactions.

Beyond their legal influence, the Ten Commandments serve as ethical touchstones for millions of people. They offer a moral compass by which individuals navigate the complexities of modern life, influencing decisions and behaviours in various contexts. The commandment to honour one's parents, for example, resonates with universal values of familial respect and responsibility, shaping personal relationships and community dynamics.

The Sabbath commandment, emphasising rest and reflection, has had a lasting impact on the concept of work-life balance, underscoring the importance of mental and spiritual well-being. In a world that increasingly values productivity and constant activity, this principle offers a counterpoint, advocating for periods of rest and rejuvenation.

The Ten Commandments have also influenced cultural narratives and educational materials, serving as foundational stories in religious and moral education. They are frequently referenced in literature, art, and media, illustrating the enduring relevance of their moral lessons in various forms of cultural expression.

These commandments have been incorporated into school curricula in various countries, often within the context of religious or moral education programs. By fostering a common set of ethical values, they contribute to the development of character and citizenship among young people, preparing them to participate constructively in diverse, multicultural societies.

Despite their widespread influence, the Ten Commandments have not been without controversy. Critics argue that their religious origins may not align with the pluralistic values of modern, secular societies, raising questions about their role in public spaces and institutions. Debates have emerged over the display of Ten Commandments monuments in public buildings and schools, highlighting the tension between religious heritage and the principles of secular governance.

Furthermore, the interpretation of these commandments in the context of contemporary moral dilemmas - such as bioethics, environmental stewardship, and digital privacy - presents challenges. As societies evolve, the application of ancient moral principles to modern issues requires thoughtful consideration and dialogue.

The Ten Commandments have undeniably shaped the moral and legal foundations of societies around the world. Their influence extends from the formulation of laws to the shaping of individual character and the strengthening of community bonds. As both a historical artefact and a living document, they continue to inspire debate, reflection, and adaptation in the face of changing societal norms and ethical challenges.

In considering the enduring influence of the Ten Commandments, it is clear that their legacy is not confined to religious or historical significance. Instead, they represent a universal set of principles that continue to guide human behaviour, inform legal standards, and enrich cultural narratives. As societies continue to evolve, the Ten Commandments remain a testament to the enduring power of ethical principles to shape human civilization.

Chapter 3.

The Heart of the Commandments: Yeshua's Approach to Living Beyond the Letter.

Yeshua had a distinctive approach to understanding and teaching the Ten Commandments, setting Him apart from most Pharisees and religious leaders of His time.

The Ten Commandments, foundational to the Jewish faith, served as a guiding light for ethical and moral living. Yet, the interpretation and application of these laws varied significantly between Yeshua and many of the Pharisees, revealing more profound insights into their spiritual ideologies and the essence of their teachings.

At the heart of Yeshua's teachings was a focus on the spirit rather than the letter of the law. He emphasised the intentions and attitudes that underlie actions, advocating for a more profound, more personal adherence to God's commandments.

This approach contrasted sharply with the Pharisees, who often stressed meticulous observance of the law's specifics. While thePharisees were concerned with outward compliance and the minutiae of rules, Yeshua called for an inward transformation that naturally expressed itself in righteous behaviour.

One of the most telling examples of their differing approaches can be seen in how they dealt with the commandment to honour the Sabbath. The Pharisees had developed an extensive list of activities prohibited on the Sabbath to safeguard its sanctity through strict regulations.

Yeshua, however, challenged this rigid interpretation. He healed the sick and performed acts of kindness on the Sabbath, actions that some Pharisees deemed unlawful. Yeshua argued that such deeds were in keeping with the Sabbath's purpose - to bring life and restoration, highlighting that legalistic interpretations should not constrain mercy and compassion.

Yeshua emphasised that the root of a person's wrongful deeds lies within their heart and mind, underscoring the profound connection between our inner thoughts and outward actions.

This perspective was clearly illustrated in his interpretation of the commandment, "You shall not murder." Yeshua expanded the traditional understanding of this rule, asserting that it not only prohibits the act of taking someone's life but also extends to the emotions of anger and contempt towards others.

According to Yeshua, harbouring such negative feelings is akin to committing the act itself, highlighting the critical importance of cultivating purity in thought to prevent wrongful actions.

This interpretation underscored His belief in the importance of purity of heart and the interconnectedness of thoughts, attitudes, and actions. In contrast, the Pharisees focused more on the physical act itself without delving into the underlying moral and spiritual dimensions that Yeshua emphasised.

Another significant point of divergence was the commandment about adultery. Yeshua expanded its meaning to include not just the physical act of infidelity but also lustful thoughts, thereby elevating the standard of moral purity to include the sanctity of the mind and heart.

This broader interpretation aimed to foster a community where relationships and personal integrity were rooted in sincere love and respect rather than merely adhering to external norms.

Yeshua's perspective on the Ten Commandments also emphasised the inseparability of love for God and love for one's neighbour. He summarised all the laws and the words of the prophets with the dual commandment to love God with all one's heart, soul, and mind and to love one's neighbour as oneself.

This summation was revolutionary, encapsulating the essence of the Ten Commandments into a call for an all-encompassing love that motivates obedience.

In contrast, the Pharisees' approach often led to a compartmentalisation of duties to God and duties to fellow humans, sometimes neglecting the latter for religious observance

.Moreover, Yeshua criticised the Pharisees for their hypocrisy and legalism. He accused them of imposing burdensome regulations on others while failing to grasp the core of the law - justice, mercy, and faithfulness.

His rebukes highlighted a fundamental difference in their understanding of living a life pleasing to God. For Yeshua, it was not about ticking off a checklist of religious duties but about embodying God's love and righteousness in every aspect of life.

In essence, Yeshua's view of the Ten Commandments invites followers to a relationship with God that transcends mere rule-following. It's a call to internalise these commandments, allowing them to shape one's character and actions from the inside out. This approach fosters a genuine transformation that reflects God's love and holiness in daily living rather than a superficial adherence to religious norms.

Contrastingly, the Pharisees' interpretation, though well-intentioned in its desire to preserve the sanctity of the law, often missed the heart of God's commandments. Their emphasis on external compliance sometimes overshadowed the deeper, relational aspects of the law that Yeshua highlighted - those of love, mercy, and sincere devotion to God.

So, we can see that Yeshua's teachings on the Ten Commandments reveal a profound understanding of their purpose - to guide individuals towards a loving and authentic relationship with God and others. His approach, emphasising the spirit of the law over its letter, challenged the prevailing religious norms and invited a more profound, more heartfelt compliance with God's will.

This perspective not only differentiated Him from the Pharisees but also offered a transformative path for His followers that leads to true righteousness and spiritual fulfilment. Through His interpretation, Yeshua underscored that the essence of the Ten Commandments is not found in rigid adherence to rules but in the cultivation of a life that radiates God's love and justice in every action and thought.

So join me on this journey through the Ten Commandments, consider what Scripture says about each of them, and see how Yeshua expanded and further defined our understanding of each.

Rather than rush through the book, I highly recommend that you study just one commandment each day, think about it, and reflect on how your thoughts and actions align with what Scripture says and what Yeshua taught.

At the end of the book (chapter 18 - Page 161) is a self-study questionnaire on each commandment with a space for notes. After reading each study, consider the four questions on the chapter you've just finished.

You may be challenged to reconsider, in the light of those, how you live your life. Whether it's by the letter of the law or the spirit of it, how your choices can affect your own life and the lives of those around you and what you might have to change.

May the Lord bless you in your studies, in your walk with Him and in your interactions with all you meet.

Chapter 4.

The First Commandment - The Foundation of Faith

I am the Lord your God, who delivered you out of the land of Egypt, out of the bonds of slavery. You are to have no other gods before me". Exodus 20:2-3.

What does Scripture tell us about having only one God?

The first commandment, found in Exodus 20:2-3, serves as a cornerstone for the understanding and practice of faith in the Old Testament. This commandment,

"I am the Lord your God, who brought you out of the land of Egypt, out of the house of bondage. You shall have no other gods before Me,"

sets the stage for the unique relationship between God and the people of Israel. It's a declaration of God's sovereignty, a reminder of His saving actions, and an imperative towards exclusive worship.

Let's explore this commandment, which at first glance may seem straightforward. But delving deeper, reveals layers of complexity as we consider its implications, and its reflections throughout the Old Testament.

We could think of it as a cosmic GPS for moral navigation, where every instruction comes from a single source, aiming to guide humanity towards a path of goodness and justice.

At its core, this commandment establishes a monotheistic framework for Israel's faith. It was a radical departure from the polytheistic cultures surrounding them, where multiple gods were worshipped for various aspects of life.

This commandment doesn't call for a blind, unthinking obedience. On the contrary, it encourages a deep, personal relationship with the divine, inviting believers to wrestle with, question, and ultimately deepen their understanding of their faith.

It's like being in a committed relationship; true depth and intimacy come from facing challenges together, not from a superficial arrangement where one's attention is divided.

The assertion *"I am the Lord your God"* identifies their God as the sole deity worthy of worship, emphasising a personal relationship characterised by fidelity and recognition of God's singular authority and benevolence.

The historical context provided, *"who brought you out of the land of Egypt, out of the house of bondage,"* serves multiple purposes.

Firstly, it anchors God's sovereignty in a recent and powerful act of deliverance, making His lordship not just a theological assertion but a demonstrated truth. This reference to the Exodus event underscores God's power, mercy, and willingness to act on behalf of His people. It's a testament to His character as a liberator and protector, themes that resonate throughout the Scriptures.

The following imperative, *"You shall have no other gods before Me,"* is both a command and a covenantal stipulation. It requires the Israelites to give undivided worship to God. The phrase *"before Me"* doesn't merely suggest a ranking but a total exclusivity. This commandment is not just about prioritising but about the exclusivity of allegiance. It challenges the Israelites to trust in God's sufficiency for all their needs, rejecting the idols and gods of neighbouring peoples.

Throughout the Old Testament, the importance of this commandment is echoed and re-echoed. The prophets, for instance, continually called Israel back to the fidelity required by this first commandment.

Idolatry, or the worship of other gods, was the primary sin the prophets railed against, illustrating how easily the Israelites drifted from this foundational command. Jeremiah 2:13, for example, sees God lamenting Israel's abandonment of Him for worthless idols, illustrating the deep betrayal of forgetting the God who saved them.

"My people have committed two evils: They have forsaken Me - the spring of living water - and they dug their own cisterns - cracked cisterns that hold no water".   Jeremiah 2:13

The narrative of the Old Testament is filled with cycles of Israel's unfaithfulness, punishment, repentance, and God's merciful deliverance, underscoring the central importance of this commandment.

The book of Judges provides a stark depiction of this cycle, showing how the Israelites' forsaking of the first commandment leads to their oppression and suffering, only to be relieved by God's intervention through judges.

In Deuteronomy, Moses reiterates the commandments to a new generation of Israelites on the verge of entering the Promised Land. Deuteronomy 6:4-5, known as the Shema, encapsulates the essence of the first commandment in a call to hear, acknowledge, and love God with all one's being.

"Hear O Israel, the Lord our God, the Lord is one. Love your God with all your heart and with all your soul and with all your strength".

This passage extends the first commandment into a total commitment of heart, soul, and might, emphasising its relational aspect. It's not merely about the avoidance of other gods but about a wholehearted devotion to the God of Israel.

Therefore, the first commandment is foundational not only to Israel's religious identity but also to their ethical and communal life. Establishing God as the sole object of worship sets forth a paradigm for understanding justice, mercy, and righteousness.

The prophets, particularly Amos and Micah, tied adherence to this commandment with social justice and ethical living, indicating that the worship of God was inseparable from righteous actions.

Moreover, the Psalms frequently celebrate God's sovereignty and deliverance, echoing the first commandment's themes. Psalms like Psalm 105 retell the Exodus story, reminding the faithful of the reasons for exclusive worship of God. These texts continually recall God's saving actions and the response of fidelity they demand.

We can see, therefore, that the first commandment is foundational to the identity and faith of the Israelites. It establishes a monotheistic belief system centred around a personal, liberating God who demands exclusive worship.

This commandment is repeatedly affirmed throughout the Old Testament, a constant reminder of God's saving actions, His sovereign lordship, and the requirement for the Israelites to live in faithful obedience. It shapes the narrative of the Israelites, guiding their historical journey and spiritual development, and remains a central tenet of their relationship with God.

Through prophets, laws, and worship, the Old Testament encapsulates the profound significance of this commandment, highlighting its pivotal role in the covenant relationship between

God and His people.

This call is an invitation to enter into a relationship with the Divine marked by exclusivity, devotion, and ethical living. It challenges believers to consider the depth of their allegiance, the integrity of their moral compass, and the sincerity of their engagement with the Divine.

The First Commandment's proclamation of monotheism resonates far beyond its ancient origins, touching on universal themes of faith, morality, and community. It calls on individuals to acknowledge a single, supreme God, shaping their spiritual outlook, ethical conduct, and communal life.

While simple in its demand, this directive is profound in its implications, offering a path towards a deeper, more meaningful engagement with the Divine and one another. It reminds us that, sometimes, the most potent truths call us to a singular focus, challenging us to look beyond the surface and find the divine spark within ourselves and the world around us.

What did Yeshua teach about having one God?

The teachings of Yeshua on faith and devotion to God, as well as the prioritisation of spiritual over material concerns, are deeply embedded in the Messianic Jewish and Christian traditions.

These teachings, foundational to the beliefs of millions worldwide, encourage followers to cultivate a profound relationship with the Divine, emphasising the importance of love, faith, and devotion above earthly treasures.

Now we explore Yeshua's perspective on the First Commandment and his guidance towards a life led by spiritual values, and we look at the Scriptures illuminating his message.

At the heart of Yeshua's teachings is the First Commandment, which he reaffirms as the greatest commandment:

"Love the Lord your God with all your heart and with all your soul and with all your mind" Matthew 22:37.

This commandment encapsulates the essence of Yeshua's message - unwavering devotion to God. It is a call to love God completely, beyond mere obedience or ritualistic worship, highlighting the importance of a personal, heartfelt connection with the Divine. This relationship is not based on fear or obligation but on love, marking the cornerstone of faith and devotion in a believer's life.

Yeshua's teachings frequently contrasted the spiritual with the material, urging his followers to prioritise their spiritual well-being over worldly possessions. One of the most poignant examples is Matthew 6:24, where he states,

"No one can serve two masters. Either you will hate the one and love the other, or you will be devoted to the one and despise the other. You cannot serve both God and money."

This vividly illustrates the incompatibility of divided loyalties between spiritual devotion and material accumulation. Yeshua warns against allowing the pursuit of wealth to become a master that detracts from one's relationship with God, underlining the transient nature of material possessions compared to the eternal value of spiritual wealth.

Another profound teaching that emphasises the importance of spiritual priorities is the parable of the rich fool (Luke 12:16-21). In this parable, a wealthy man decides to tear down his barns and build bigger ones to store his surplus grain, planning to relax, eat, drink, and be merry thereafter. God, however, calls him a fool because that very night, his life would be demanded from him, and he would not be able to take his earthly wealth with him beyond death. As the saying goes, there are no pockets in a shroud.

This parable is a stark reminder that life's value is not measured by material abundance but by one's relationship with God and the treasures accumulated in heaven.

Yeshua also emphasised the necessity of faith in God's provision, further illustrating his teaching on prioritising the spiritual over the material.

In the Sermon on the Mount, he assures his listeners that God knows their needs and will provide for them, saying,

"Therefore I tell you, do not worry about your life, what you will eat or drink; or about your body, what you will wear. Isn't life more than food and the body more than clothes?... But seek first his kingdom and righteousness, and all these things will also be given to you"

Matthew 6:25, 33.

This teaching encourages a reliance on God's provision and a focus on spiritual pursuits, promising that material needs will be met due to such faith.

This concept of storing treasures in heaven rather than on earth is a cornerstone of Yeshua's teachings on spiritual priorities. He advises,

"Do not store up for yourselves treasures on earth, where moths and vermin destroy, and where thieves break in and steal. But store up for yourselves treasures in heaven, where moths and vermin do not destroy, and where thieves do not break in and steal"

Matthew 6:19-20.

This teaching is a metaphor for the impermanence of material wealth and the enduring nature of spiritual achievements, encouraging followers to invest in what is eternally significant.

In essence, Yeshua's teachings on the First Commandment and prioritising spiritual over material values offer a comprehensive guide for living a life of faith, love, and devotion to God. He clearly shows what it means to truly love God with all one's heart, soul, and mind, emphasising the importance of spiritual wealth over earthly possessions.

Through parables, direct teachings, and his living example, Yeshua demonstrates the transformative power of prioritising one's relationship with God, assuring that such devotion leads to a life of fulfilment, purpose, and eternal significance.

In a world increasingly driven by materialism and the pursuit of wealth, Yeshua's teachings remain profoundly counter-cultural, offering a radical alternative that values the spiritual over the material.

They challenge individuals to examine their priorities, encouraging a life led by spiritual values such as love, faith, and devotion to God. By embodying these teachings, followers of Yeshua are invited to navigate the complexities of life with a focus on the eternal, cultivating a relationship with God that transcends the temporary allure of worldly possessions.

Yeshua's teachings on the First Commandment and the importance of spiritual over material concerns provide a timeless blueprint for a deep faith and devoted life. Through scriptural quotes and parables, he vividly illustrates the value of prioritising one's relationship with God, encouraging followers to seek spiritual riches that endure beyond this earthly life.

In doing so, Yeshua offers a pathway to true fulfilment that elevates love for God and the pursuit of spiritual growth, guiding followers towards a life marked by divine purpose and eternal significance.

How can we follow Yeshua's teaching about having one God in the modern world?

The First Commandment, often cited as *"Thou shalt have no other gods before me,"* is not merely a directive towards monotheism but a profound foundation for personal integrity. This commandment urges believers to prioritise their allegiance to God above all else.

However, when we peel back the layers, its implications for personal integrity extend far beyond the religious sphere, offering timeless wisdom on living a life of authenticity, purpose, and moral fortitude.

To fully grasp the First Commandment's impact on personal integrity, it's essential to understand its primary message. This commandment doesn't simply forbid the worship of other deities; it calls for an undivided heart and loyalty.

It's about prioritising what's truly important, urging individuals to align their values, actions, and lives around a central, unshakeable core. For believers, this core is their faith in God, but the principle of having a guiding centre is universally applicable.

Personal integrity is an inner compass that guides our thoughts, actions, and decisions. It's a consistent character that remains steadfast regardless of external pressures or temptations. In emphasising a singular devotion, the First Commandment mirrors the call for a unified self, where our beliefs, values, and actions align.

At its heart, the First Commandment challenges us to be authentic. Maintaining authenticity requires being clear about what we stand for in a world brimming with distractions, temptations, and pressures to conform. This clarity comes from recognising and committing to our core values, much like the exclusive devotion to God outlined in the commandments. Authenticity means our actions are not swayed by the latest trends or the approval of others but are rooted in our deepest convictions.

The commandment also embodies the courage to stand alone. It acknowledges that true devotion - whether to a deity or a set of principles - often demands going against the grain. Personal integrity involves making choices that are not always popular or easy but are right. It's about having the moral fortitude to uphold our standards, even when doing so might lead to criticism, isolation, or sacrifice. This aspect of the First Commandment reminds us that integrity often requires courage and resilience.

The biblical mandate to have "no other gods" suggests a wholeness of being, a life undivided by conflicting loyalties or desires. This wholeness is a cornerstone of personal integrity. It's about being the same person in public and private, ensuring our lives are not fragmented but integrated around our core principles. This integration makes us reliable, trustworthy, and consistent - essential for meaningful relationships and purposeful life.

Living a life of integrity, as outlined by the First Commandment, has profound ripple effects. It shapes our character and influences our relationships, communities, and the broader world. When we live with integrity, we build trust. Others know they can rely on us to be honest, consistent, and true to our word. This trust is the foundation of strong, healthy relationships. Just as the First Commandment calls for a reliable devotion to God, personal integrity fosters reliability and trustworthiness in our interactions with others.

Personal integrity also positions us as moral leaders, regardless of our official roles or titles. By living in alignment with our core values and principles, we set an example for others. This leadership isn't about power or authority but about inspiring and influencing those around us through our actions and choices.

Lastly, integrity brings inner peace. A profound tranquillity comes from knowing our lives are built on a solid foundation of principles we genuinely believe in. This peace is akin to the spiritual fulfilment the First Commandment seeks to provide through a devoted relationship with God. When our external actions match our internal convictions, we live in harmony with ourselves.

While religious in nature, the First Commandment offers universal wisdom on the importance of personal integrity. It calls us to live lives centred around our deepest convictions, to be authentic and courageous, and to maintain a consistency of character that withstands the test of time and trial. Doing so ensures our peace of mind, enhances our relationships, establishes us as moral leaders, and contributes to a more trustworthy and cohesive society.

Thus, the First Commandment's implications for personal integrity are profound, urging us towards a life of purpose, dignity, and unwavering commitment to our core values.

Chapter 5.

The Second Commandment - Idolatry in the modern age.

"You shall not make for yourself a carved image - any likeness of anything that is in heaven above, or that is in the earth beneath, or that is in the water under the earth; you shall not bow down to them nor serve them. For I, the LORD your God, am a jealous God, visiting the iniquity of the fathers upon the children to the third and fourth generations of those who hate Me, but showing mercy to thousands, to those who love Me and keep My commandments."

What does Scripture tell us about Idolatry?

The second of the Ten Commandments, represents a fundamental aspect of the Old Testament's teachings on worship and idolatry. This commandment provides a clear directive against the creation and worship of idols.

This commandment is not merely a prohibition against idolatry but a foundational principle that guides the faithful in understanding the nature of their relationship with God.

From a Scriptural perspective, idol worship is a concept that extends far beyond the mere act of venerating statues or images. It entails any form of devotion, reverence, or trust in anything or anyone other than the one true God, as revealed in the Bible.

This concept is woven throughout the fabric of both the Old and New Testaments, providing a comprehensive view of God's singularity and supremacy and the human inclination towards idolatry.

In the Old Testament, the prohibition against idol worship is foundational to the covenantal relationship between God and the Israelites. The Ten Commandments establish this relationship's legal and moral framework. The first commandment explicitly states,

"You shall have no other gods before me" (Exodus 20:3),

setting the tone for God's unique and exclusive worship. The subsequent command against making and venerating graven images underscores the seriousness with which God views idolatry.

This prohibition is not merely a warning against the creation of physical objects of worship but a directive against attributing divine power or honour to anything other than God

The essence of this commandment lies in its explicit rejection of idol worship. In the ancient Near East, the practice of idolatry was commonplace among the nations surrounding Israel. These idols, often crafted from wood, stone, or metal, represented the pantheon of gods and goddesses worshipped by these cultures.

The God of Israel, however, distinguishes Himself from these deities by forbidding the creation of any physical representation for worship. This prohibition underscores the transcendence and invisibility of God, who cannot be contained or represented by any material form.

The rationale behind this commandment is multifaceted. Firstly, it emphasises the uniqueness and sovereignty of God. By forbidding the creation of idols, the commandment rejects the polytheistic tendencies of the time, affirming the monotheistic belief in one, supreme God. This distinction was crucial for the identity and religious practice of the Israelites, setting them apart from their neighbours.

Secondly, the commandment addresses the nature of God's

relationship with His people. It speaks to the intimacy and exclusivity of this relationship, where God is not just a deity to be appeased through images or rituals but is a living, personal being who engages directly with His people. This relationship is built on love, trust, and obedience, not on the manipulation of divine powers through idols.

The warning of consequences for those who disobey this commandment illustrates the seriousness with which God views idolatry. The mention of visiting *"the iniquity of the fathers upon the children to the third and fourth generations of those who hate Me"*

highlights the communal and generational impact of sin.

It suggests that the repercussions of idolatry extend beyond the individual, affecting families and communities across generations. This aspect of the commandment underlines the belief in the social and moral fabric of society being deeply influenced by religious fidelity or infidelity.

Conversely, the promise of mercy

"to thousands, to those who love Me and keep My commandments"

reveals God's enduring love and faithfulness. This contrast between punishment and mercy serves not only as a deterrent against idolatry but also as an invitation to a life of faithfulness and devotion to God. It assures the faithful of God's boundless grace and mercy towards those who love Him and adhere to His commandments.

The significance of this commandment is further explored in various parts of the Old Testament. For instance, the narratives of the Israelites' frequent lapses into idol worship, such as the golden calf incident (Exodus 32), and the subsequent consequences, reinforce the importance of this commandment. These stories serve as cautionary tales, illustrating the devastating effects of idolatry on the individual and communal relationship with God.

Moreover, the prophets often echoed the themes of the second commandment in their calls for repentance and return to faithful worship of God. For example, Isaiah's denunciation of idolatry (Isaiah 44:9-20) powerfully critiques the incredible stupidity of crafting and worshipping idols, emphasising the incomparability and sovereignty of God.

The Lord said: "Those people who make idols are nothing themselves, and the idols they treasure are just as worthless. Worshipers of idols are blind, stupid, and foolish. Why make an idol or an image that can't do a thing? Everyone who makes idols and all who worship them are mere humans, who will end up sadly disappointed. Let them face me in court and be terrified.

A metalworker shapes an idol by using a hammer and heat from the fire. In his powerful hand he holds a hammer, as he pounds the metal into the proper shape. But he gets hungry and thirsty and loses his strength.

Some woodcarvers measure a piece of wood, then draw an outline. The idol is carefully carved with each detail exact. At last it looks like a person and is placed in a temple. Either cedar, cypress, oak, or any tree from the forest may be chosen. Or even a pine tree planted by the woodcarver and watered by the rain. Some of the wood is used to make a fire for heating or for cooking. One piece is made into an idol, then the woodcarver bows down and worships it. He enjoys the warm fire and the meat that was roasted over the burning coals. Afterwards, he bows down to worship the wooden idol. "Protect me!" he says. "You are my god."

Those who worship idols are stupid and blind! They don't have enough sense to say to themselves, "I made a fire with half of the wood and cooked my bread and meat on it. Then I made something worthless with the other half. Why worship a block of wood?" How can anyone be stupid enough to trust something that can be burned to ashes? No one can save themselves like that. Don't they realise that the idols they hold in their hands are not really gods?"

These prophetic teachings, while reiterating the prohibition against idolatry, also highlight the hope of restoration and reconciliation with God for those who turn away from idols and seek Him sincerely.

In summary, the second commandment is a cornerstone of Old Testament theology, encapsulating the essential principles of worship, the nature of God, and the dynamics of the divine-human relationship. It starkly contrasts the worship of the living, invisible God with the practices of idolatry prevalent in the surrounding cultures.

This commandment not only prohibits the creation and worship of physical idols but also invites the faithful into a deeper, more personal relationship with God.

Through its warnings and promises, it underscores the consequences of idolatry while affirming the steadfast love and mercy of God for those who remain faithful to Him. The enduring relevance of this commandment lies in its call to recognize and worship God in His transcendent uniqueness and sovereignty, fostering a relationship grounded in love, obedience, and devotion.

What did Yeshua teach about idolatry?

Idol worship is a topic that has been addressed extensively in religious texts. Yeshua discussed this issue in a deeply interconnected way with the Ten Commandments, specifically focusing on the first two. These commandments, given to Moses on Mount Sinai, serve as a foundational element in understanding the nature of idolatry and its implications in a spiritual and everyday context.

The first commandment,

"You shall have no other gods before me,"

directly addresses the concept of idolatry by forbidding the worship of any entity other than God. The second commandment,

"You shall not make for yourself an image in the form of anything in heaven above or on the earth beneath or in the waters below. You shall not bow down to them or worship them,"

expands on this prohibition by explicitly forbidding the creation and worship of physical representations or idols.

Yeshua's teachings often revisited the themes of these commandments, emphasising the importance of devotion to God alone. In the Gospels, His messages about idol worship can be interpreted in the literal sense of worshipping statues or icons and, in a broader sense, including anything that takes priority over one's relationship with God.

One of the fundamental aspects of Yeshua's teaching is the emphasis on the heart's allegiance. In Matthew 22:37-38, Yeshua cites the Shema from Deuteronomy 6:5, saying,

"Love the Lord your God with all your heart and soul and with all your mind. This is the first and greatest commandment."

This directive underlines the essence of avoiding idolatry - devotion to God with an undivided heart.

Idolatry, in its broader interpretation, can be seen as placing anything - be it wealth, power, relationships, or even one's ego -

above the primacy of God. Yeshua often warned against allowing these worldly things to dominate our lives.

For example, in the parable of the rich young man, Yeshua illustrates how material wealth can quickly become an idol, preventing the young man from fully following Him.

And behold, a man approached him, saying, "Teacher, what good deed must I do to have eternal life?" And he said to him, "Why do you ask me about what is good? There is only one who is good. If you would enter life, keep the commandments." He said to him, "Which ones?" And Yeshua said, "You shall not murder, You shall not commit adultery, You shall not steal, You shall not bear false witness, Honour your father and mother, and You shall love your neighbour as yourself." The young man said to him, "All these I have kept. What do I still lack?" Yeshua told him, "If you would be perfect, go, sell what you possess and give to the poor, and you will have treasure in heaven; and come, follow me." When the young man heard this, he left sorrowfully, for he had great possessions. And Yeshua said to his disciples, "Truly, I say to you, only with difficulty will a rich person enter the kingdom of heaven."
Matthew 19:16-23

Moreover, Yeshua's actions, such as cleansing the temple, symbolise His disdain for practices that pervert sincere worship. The temple, which should have been a place of devout worship, had been turned into a marketplace, showing how even religious practices could become idolatrous when they lose their proper focus.

Yeshua entered the temple courts and drove out all those selling and buying in the temple. He overturned the money changers' tables and the seats of those selling doves. He told them, "It is written, 'My house will be called a house of prayer,' but you are making it a den of robbers!"
Matthew 21:12-13

The overlap between the first and second commandments is significant because they both deal with the orientation of the human heart and soul. While the first commandment deals with the object of worship (God alone), the second commandment addresses the manner and means of worship, prohibiting the creation of physical idols.

Together, they encapsulate the essence of monotheism and the purity of worship that Yeshua advocated. Yeshua's teachings and actions constantly emphasised the heart's intention and the need for a personal, genuine relationship with God. He taught that the outward act of worship is meaningless if it is not rooted in true love and reverence for God. This is evident in His critique of the Pharisees, whom He accused of honouring God only with their lips.

"These people honour me with their lips, but their heart is far from me. Matthew 15:8.

The relevance of Yeshua's teachings on idol worship extends beyond the first-century context into today's world, where modern idols can be as subtle as they are pervasive. In a society where success, materialism, and self-gratification often take precedence, Yeshua's message remains a poignant reminder of the need for spiritual vigilance.

Understanding idolatry from Yeshua's perspective also involves recognising the subtle ways in which idolatrous attitudes can infiltrate our lives. They could be excessively preoccupied with career advancement, have an unhealthy attachment to their image and reputation, or even have an obsessive dedication to certain ideologies or political beliefs. While not inherently wrong, these things become problematic when they occupy the place in our hearts that should be reserved for God.

Yeshua's discourse on idolatry is not just about forbidding specific actions but is deeply rooted in transforming the human heart. His call to worship God alone is a call to a transformative relationship that prioritises divine love and obedience above all else. According to Yeshua's teachings, this relationship is the antithesis of idol worship and is the foundation of a life following God's will.

Yeshua's teachings on idol worship, as reflected in the discussions around the first and second commandments, provide a comprehensive understanding of the nature of idolatry. He emphasised the importance of loving God with an undivided heart and warned against allowing anything to usurp God's place in our lives. This timeless message challenges us to reflect on our daily priorities and worship. It is a call to introspection and realignment, urging us to evaluate and ensure that our worship and devotion are directed towards the one true God, in spirit and truth.

How can we follow Yeshua's teaching on idolatry in the modern world?

Following Yeshua's teachings on avoiding idolatry in the modern world can seem daunting, especially when idolatry has morphed into many forms that are not always easy to recognise.

Yeshua taught extensively about worshipping God alone and not allowing anything to take His place in our lives. In the current age, idolatry might not look like the golden calves of the past, but it manifests in ways that can be just as spiritually destructive.

Let's recap what idolatry means. Traditionally, it's the worship of physical idols or gods, but in a broader sense, it's giving ultimate value and priority to something other than God. In today's context, this can be anything from money, career, relationships, technology, or even one's ego or image. Yeshua's teaching on idolatry urges us to keep our hearts and minds focused on God and His commandments, ensuring that nothing else takes precedence over that relationship.

Money is a common idol in the modern world. Yeshua warned about the dangers of serving money rather than God, highlighting the impossibility of serving two masters. This is evident in the relentless pursuit of wealth and material success, often at the expense of spiritual well-being, ethical behaviour, and relationships.

To follow Yeshua's teaching here, one must adopt a mindset that views money and resources as means to serve God and others rather than as ends in themselves. Practically, this could mean prioritising charitable giving, avoiding unethical financial practices, and ensuring that pursuing wealth doesn't overshadow one's spiritual and relational commitments.

In the realm of relationships, idolatry can occur when one's partner, children, or friendships become the ultimate focus, sidelining God's place in one's life. Yeshua emphasised loving God with all one's heart, soul, and mind as the greatest commandment, which means that while relationships are important, they should not overshadow one's devotion to God. Balancing this involves nurturing relationships that honour God, using them to foster love, respect, and mutual growth in faith rather than allowing them to become sources of obsession or control.

Technology, particularly social media, is a modern-day idol that can consume vast amounts of time and attention. It often leads to comparing oneself with others, striving for likes and validation, or becoming engrossed in a digital life at the expense of real-world relationships and spiritual growth.

To follow Yeshua's teachings in this area, one needs to practise self-control and discernment, using technology as a positive connection and information tool rather than letting it dominate one's life. It's about creating healthy boundaries, where time spent in prayer, meditation, and community precedes digital engagement.

Even one's image or ego can become an idol. In a world that often promotes self-aggrandisement and personal success as the ultimate goals, it's easy to fall into the trap of idolising oneself.

Yeshua taught humility and servitude as the paths to true greatness, calling for followers to seek God's approval rather than human validation. This means living a service life, focusing on loving others as oneself and seeking to reflect God's love in all actions rather than being driven by a desire for fame or recognition.

In all these examples, the common thread is the need to keep God at the centre of our lives, ensuring that other things do not usurp His place. This requires regular self-examination and reflection, honesty about our priorities, and conscious choices to align our lives with Yeshua's teachings. Given the myriad distractions and temptations in the modern world, it's not always easy, but it is deeply rewarding and transformative.

Following Yeshua's path in avoiding idolatry also involves engaging in practices that foster a solid spiritual foundation. Regular prayer, reading scriptures, and participating in communal worship can help maintain focus on God and His will. These practices provide strength and guidance to navigate the complexities of modern life while staying true to spiritual principles.

Moreover, Yeshua's approach to idolatry was not just about avoidance but also about transformation. He taught that replacing idolatrous attachments with love for God and neighbours leads to a fulfilled and purposeful life. This means actively seeking ways to serve others, being generous with time, resources, and talents, and living out the values of the Kingdom of God in everyday life.

Community plays a crucial role in this journey. Being part of a faith community provides support, accountability, and inspiration to live according to Yeshua's teachings. It allows for sharing experiences, learning from others, and growing together in faith. In these communities, stories of overcoming modern-day idols can be shared, offering encouragement and practical insights into navigating the challenges of maintaining a God-centred life in a world of distractions.

However, it's important to recognise that idolatry is often a matter of the heart, and what becomes an idol for one person may not be for another. This subjective nature of idolatry calls for a personal relationship with God, guided by the Holy Spirit, to discern where idolatrous tendencies may lie in one's own life. It's a personal journey of growth, learning, and continual surrender to God's will.

To summarise, following Yeshua's teachings on avoiding idolatry in the modern world is more than just steering clear of obvious false gods. It's about examining our lives to see where we might place other things above God, whether money, relationships, technology or even our image.

It's a call to live intentionally, with God as the central focus, guided by practices that nurture our spiritual health and supported by a community that shares this commitment. By doing so, we can navigate the complexities of modern life with wisdom and grace, staying true to the teachings of Yeshua and living out our faith in a genuine and impactful way.

Chapter 6.

The Third Commandment - The power of words.

*"You shall not take the name of the L*ORD *your God in vain, for the Lord will not hold him guiltless who takes His name in vain.*

What does Scripture tell us about using the name of the Lord?

"Thou shalt not take the name of the Lord thy God in vain" is the third of the ten foundational commandments given to Moses on Mount Sinai, embedded deeply within Judeo-Christian tradition's spiritual and moral fibres. This directive, found in Exodus 20:7, is more than just a rule about language; it's about respect, relationship, and the essence of holiness.

To fully understand the scope of this commandment, we should explore the historical context, the linguistic implications, and the spiritual significance.

The name of God, in biblical times, was not merely a label or identifier, as names are often considered today. It carried the weight of the individual's character, essence, and presence. God's name was sacred for the Israelites, embodying his power, presence, and promise. Therefore, using God's name in vain wasn't just a matter of misusing a word; it was misrepresenting the very nature of the divine.

The term "vain," or "shav" in Hebrew, suggests emptiness, falsehood, and futility, broadening the commandment's scope to encompass false oaths, deceitful promises, and actions that compromise the sanctity of God's name. Leviticus 19:12 explicitly cautions against swearing falsely by God's name, equating such acts with profanity, or treating the sacred disrespectfully.

The commandment, therefore, prohibits using God's name in a way that is empty, frivolous, or insincere, extending to false promises, careless expressions, and manipulative actions in God's name.

In the broader context of Scripture, God's name holds a place of ultimate reverence. The Psalms, for instance, are filled with verses that highlight the power and sanctity of God's name. Psalm 29:2 commands,

"Give unto the Lord the glory due unto his name; worship the Lord in the beauty of holiness."

This suggests that the name of God is inherently holy and deserving of respect and honour.

The misuse of God's name reflects not just a linguistic error but a deeper spiritual misalignment. In biblical narratives, names are significant; they often define a person's destiny or character.

For example, Abraham means "father of many nations," reflecting his role in God's plan. When it comes to God, his names encompass his omnipotence, omniscience, and omnipresence, representing his divine attributes. Therefore, to take his name in vain is to disregard the very essence of who God is.

The prohibition of taking God's name in vain also encompasses false oaths and perjury, where God's name is invoked to lend credibility to a lie or a deceitful promise. In Leviticus 19:12, it is written,

"And you shall not swear by my name falsely, neither will you profane the name of your God: I am the LORD."

This underscores the idea that God's name should not be entangled with dishonesty or deceit, as it degrades the sacredness of the divine.

Moreover, this commandment is about maintaining the integrity of one's relationship with God. Using God's name in vain can be seen as an abuse of the relationship, taking God's ever-present support and love for granted. It signifies a lack of fear and respect for God, leading to a breakdown in the spiritual communion that should be nurtured with reverence and sincerity.

The concept of not using the Lord's name in vain extends beyond mere speech. It encompasses the way we live. By living in a way that honours God's name, individuals reflect God's character in the world.

When Messianic Jews and Christians, for instance, identify with the Saviour, they carry his name with their identity. Their actions, therefore, should reflect the character and teachings of Yeshua, not to take his name in vain through their conduct.

In the wisdom literature of the Bible, such as Proverbs, the use and reverence of God's name are linked with wisdom and ethical living. Proverbs 30:8-9 speaks of not taking God's name in vain in the context of living righteously and honestly, associating the misuse of God's name with deceit and falsehood.

"Keep falsehood and futility far from me, and give me neither poverty nor wealth. Provide just the food I need today, for if I have too much, I might deny you and say, "Who is God?" And if I am poor, I might steal and so profane the name of my God".

Throughout history, the interpretation of what it means to take God's name in vain has evolved. Yet, the core message remains consistent: God's name represents his divine being and should be treated with the highest respect and reverence. This commandment reminds believers of the power of speech and the importance of using words to reflect the sacredness of the divine.

In practical terms, avoiding misusing God's name means more than just refraining from swearing or blasphemy. It means engaging with God and speaking of God in ways that are thoughtful, respectful, and sincere. It's about recognising the power of God's name to invoke his presence, promise, and power.

The commandment against taking God's name in vain is a constant reminder to uphold the sanctity of the divine in speech and action.It calls for a conscious effort to respect and honour the profound relationship between the divine and the human. In a broader sense, it's a call to integrity and truthfulness, ensuring that one's words and actions are aligned with the reverence due to God.

The commandment

"You shalt not take the name of the Lord your God in vain"

is a directive that touches on legal, ethical, and spiritual realms. It's not just about avoiding certain words but embracing a lifestyle of reverence, integrity, and respect for the divine.

It invites a deeper reflection on how we represent and relate to the divine essence, ensuring that God's name is handled with the care and respect it deserves. Through understanding and adhering to this commandment, individuals are encouraged to foster a sincere and respectful relationship with the divine, reflecting its sanctity in every aspect of their lives.

What did Yeshua teach about taking the Lord's name in vain?

One aspect of Yeshua's teachings encapsulated within the Ten

Commandments is the directive against taking the Lord's name in vain. This commandment, found in Exodus 20:7, is typically understood as a prohibition against using God's name disrespectfully or frivolously. However, Yeshua's interpretation and application of this commandment are much more profound, revealing a richness of spiritual and moral guidance.

To grasp the depth of what Yeshua taught about taking the Lord's name in vain, it's crucial to understand the context in which he lived and taught. He emerged in a society where the Law of Moses was the daily life and spiritual practice bedrock. People were keenly aware of the laws and their outward observances.

Yet, Yeshua frequently pointed out that mere outward compliance with the law was insufficient. He sought to draw people's attention to the spirit behind the law, emphasising the heart's condition over external actions.

Regarding the specific teaching on not taking the Lord's name in vain, Yeshua did not address it in a direct, standalone statement as he did with other commandments. Instead, he wove the principle into his broader teachings on sincerity, respect, and the sanctity of speech. For Yeshua, words carried immense power and reflected one's inner being. In Matthew 12:34-37, he states,

"For out of the abundance of the heart the mouth speaks... for by your words, you will be justified, and by your words, you will be condemned."

This connection between heart, speech, and spiritual condition underscores that taking the Lord's name in vain goes beyond mere speech - it's about the state of one's heart and the intention behind one's words. Yeshua's teaching method often challenged the prevailing interpretations of the law, pushing his listeners beyond the literal text to the ethical and spiritual implications.

For example, in the Sermon on the Mount, he expands on the commandments, intensifying them and internalising their applications. Although he doesn't refer directly to the commandment about taking the Lord's name in vain here, the underlying principle of sincerity and truthfulness in one's relationship with God and others is thoroughly ingrained in his message.

By emphasising integrity and authenticity, Yeshua implied that taking the Lord's name in vain could occur in ways beyond speech. It could happen through living a life that professed allegiance to God but denied him through actions.

This hypocrisy was something he vehemently opposed, as seen in his harsh critiques of the scribes and Pharisees, whom he accused of honouring God with their lips while their hearts were far from him (Matthew 15:8). In this light, taking the Lord's name in vain also involves representing God falsely or claiming his authority in matters where one does not follow or believe in his teachings.

Furthermore, Yeshua's interactions and parables often illustrated the gravity of making vows or oaths carelessly in God's name, which was another form of taking the Lord's name in vain. He taught that one's yes should simply be yes, and no, no, as in Matthew 5:37.

"Let what you say be simply 'Yes' or 'No'; anything more than this comes from evil".

This instruction stresses the importance of being truthful and reliable without having to swear by God's name, highlighting that the misuse of God's name to guarantee one's honesty was unnecessary and even deceitful.

The essence of Yeshua's teaching on this matter is profoundly tied to the authenticity of one's faith and the consistency between one's words and actions. He called for a personal, genuine relationship with God reflected in every aspect of life, including how one uses God's name and speaks of spiritual matters.

This depth of sincerity ensures that God's name is treated with the utmost respect and honour, not just in specific instances of speech but in the totality of one's life and actions.

Yeshua emphasised the importance of speech and how it affects our spiritual and community life. In the Gospel of John, Yeshua is described as the *"Word made flesh,"* showing a deep link between God's divine word and our words. This idea stresses the power of speech, including how using God's name influences our reality and relationships with God and other people.

One must also consider the broader narrative of his life and teachings to understand what Yeshua taught about taking the Lord's name in vain. He often focused on the love of God and neighbour as the greatest commandments, which encompass and fulfil the law.

In this context, using God's name in a way that contradicts love, respect, and reverence for God and others is a clear violation of the commandment, as understood by Yeshua. His teachings and actions consistently pointed to a way of life where every word and deed is infused with the consciousness of God's presence and reverence for his name.

So, Yeshua's teachings on taking the Lord's name in vain offer a nuanced and profound perspective that transcends a mere prohibition of misuse in speech. He presented a holistic view of living in a manner that honours God's name through integrity, authenticity, and love.

His approach was not about following a rule just for rule-following sake but nurturing a deep, heartfelt relationship with the Divine that naturally respects and upholds the sanctity of God's name. In this way, Yeshua taught that the commandment is not just a linguistic guideline but a call to live a life consistently aligned with the values and character of the God whose name we bear and proclaim.

How should we follow Yeshua's teaching about not taking the Lord's name in vain in the modern world?

In today's fast-paced world, where words often fly faster than thoughts, the teaching of Yeshua about not taking the Lord's name in vain holds a profound significance. This commandment, rooted in the Ten Commandments given to Moses on Mount Sinai, is more than an injunction against swearing. It's a call to respect the sacred, live with integrity, and recognise the power of words.

To understand the depth of this teaching, we must first grasp what it means to take the Lord's name in vain. Traditionally, this was understood as a prohibition against using God's name carelessly or in a way that dishonours it. But on a deeper level, it speaks to how we represent and reflect on the divine in our daily actions and words.

In the modern context, taking the Lord's name in vain can manifest in various ways, not just through speech but through actions that contradict the values and principles that the name of God represents.

For example, when individuals claim to act in the name of God, but their actions foster hate, division, or harm, they effectively take the Lord's name in vain. It's not just about uttering God's name in anger or frustration but about the inconsistency between one's professed beliefs and actual behaviour.

In the public sphere, we often see political and social leaders who invoke God's name to justify policies or actions that, upon closer examination, seem to contravene the ethical and moral teachings associated with religious traditions. When leaders claim divine sanction for decisions that oppress or marginalise others, they misuse the sacred as a tool for their ends.

This commandment also speaks to how we interact online in the digital age. With its quickfire communication, social media often sees the casual or disrespectful invocation of the sacred. Memes, tweets, and posts may flippantly use religious references or God's name, diluting the reverence that these sacred elements demand. The anonymity and distance digital interaction provides can sometimes lead to a disconnect between our online behaviour and our spiritual values.

Moreover, the line between colloquial language and respect for the sacred can blur in everyday conversations. Phrases like "Oh my God" or "Jesus Christ" often express surprise, frustration, or excitement without considering their religious significance. While not malicious in intent, these speech habits reflect a broader cultural trend of desensitising the sacredness of divine names.

But how do we then live out this teaching in a meaningful way? First and foremost, it requires mindfulness about how we use God's name and represent our faith in our actions. Being mindful means pausing before we speak or act, considering whether our words and deeds reflect the reverence we claim to hold for the divine.

Respecting the Lord's name also means aligning our actions with the values that this name represents - love, compassion, justice, and truth. This alignment isn't just about avoiding negative behaviour but is also about actively doing good.

For instance, conducting business ethically and with integrity in the workplace reflects respect for the divine. In community life, treating others with kindness and fairness shows a commitment to the principles that the sacred name embodies.

Educating ourselves and others about the importance of this commandment can also help. In families, schools, and religious communities, teaching the meaning and significance of sacred names and the respect they deserve can foster a culture of reverence and mindfulness.

The challenge is great, especially in a world that often values speed over reflection and sensationalism over depth. But the rewards of living in a way that truly honours the sacred name are profound. It fosters a world where respect, integrity, and love are the cornerstones of individual and communal life.

So, following Yeshua's teaching about not taking the Lord's name in vain is much more than avoiding certain words or phrases. It's about living a life that reflects the sanctity and love that the name of God embodies.

We must honour the divine in our conversations, actions, and hearts. This commitment to living in reverence of the sacred is not just for the benefit of our spiritual well-being but also for nurturing a world where respect and integrity prevail.

By embodying the values that the Lord's name represents, we contribute to a culture that cherishes the sacred and lives out the profound teachings of Yeshua in meaningful and transformative ways.

Chapter 7.

The Fourth Commandment. A day apart - The importance of rest, reflection and renewal

"Remember the Sabbath day, to keep it holy. Six days you shall labour and do all your work, but the seventh day is the Sabbath of the LORD your God. In it, you shall do no work: you, nor your son, nor your daughter, nor your male servant, nor your female servant, nor your cattle, nor your stranger who is within your gates. For in six days, the LORD made the heavens, the earth, the sea, and all that is in them, and rested the seventh day. Therefore, the LORD blessed the Sabbath day and hallowed it".

What does Scripture tell us about keeping the Shabbat?

In the rich mosaic of spiritual practices across the world, the concept of Shabbat, or Sabbath, holds a unique place, especially within the rich traditions of Judaism. This day of rest, which spans from Friday evening to Saturday evening, is not just a time to pause from the week's labours but also a profound opportunity to reconnect with the divine, with oneself, and with the essence of life. But what does Scripture really say about keeping the Shabbat?

At the heart of the Shabbat concept is the Creation story itself, where God, after crafting the universe in six days, took a step back on the seventh day to rest. This is not just a whimsical anecdote; it's foundational to understanding why Shabbat exists. The Book of Genesis describes God blessing the seventh day and making it holy because on it God rested from all the work of creating that had been done.

On the seventh day, God finished his work and rested from all his work. God blessed the seventh day and set it apart as holy because on it he rested from all his work of creation.   Genesis 2:2-3

This divine rest sets a precedent, not because the Almighty needed to catch a breath, but as a model for us to follow: a cycle of work and rest that is both natural and necessary.

Exodus 20:8-11 and Deuteronomy 5:12-15 serve up the commandments about the Shabbat with slightly different garnishes, but the core message is consistent: Remember the Shabbat day by keeping it holy. Six days you shall labour and do all your work, but the seventh day is a Shabbat to the Lord your God. On it, you shall not do any work.

The rationale in Exodus points back to the Creation narrative, emphasising rest and holiness, while Deuteronomy adds a layer of social justice, reminding the Israelites of their past bondage in Egypt and instructing them to allow their servants and animals to rest as well. Here, the Shabbat is not just a personal pause but a communal one, where rest extends to all corners of society, emphasising equality and compassion.

But Scripture doesn't stop at just commanding rest; it wraps the Shabbat in layers of meaning and practice. For instance, in Exodus, the Shabbat is described as a sign between God and the Israelites, a perpetual covenant to be observed for generations.

"Speak to the people of Israel. Tell them, 'You must observe my Shabbats diligently, because the Shabbat is a sign between me and you throughout your generations, so that you may know that I am the Lord, who sets you apart as holy. So you shall observe the Shabbat, for it is holy to you. Everyone who profanes it must certainly be put to death, for if anyone does any work on the Shabbat, his life shall be cut off from among his people. On six days work may be done, but the seventh day is a Shabbat of complete rest, holy to the Lord. Whoever does any work on the Shabbat day must certainly be put to death. Therefore the people of Israel shall observe the Shabbat by keeping the Shabbat throughout their generations as a perpetual covenant. It is a permanent sign between me and the people of Israel, for in six

days the Lord made heaven and earth, and on the seventh day he rested and was refreshed.'"   Exodus 31:13-17

It's a day that sanctifies, a reminder of the divine act of creation and God's ongoing relationship with His people. The passage also carries a stern warning about desecrating the Shabbat, underscoring its sanctity and importance in the spiritual and communal life of the Israelites.

Then there's the prophetic angle, where Isaiah 58:13-14 offers a refreshing perspective on the Shabbat, framing it not just as an obligation but as a delight.

"But first, you must start respecting the Shabbat as a joyful day of worship. You must stop doing and saying whatever you please on this special day. Then you will truly enjoy knowing the L<small>ORD</small>*. He will let you rule from the highest mountains and bless you with the land of your ancestor Jacob. The* L<small>ORD</small> *has spoken!"*

The prophet calls for respecting the day by avoiding one's own interests and conversations, and instead, honouring God. In return, the Lord promises joy and fulfilment, highlighting the Shabbat as a day of spiritual enrichment and divine connection, rather than mere rest from physical labour.

It's interesting to note how Shabbat is more than just a day off in the biblical context. It's an institution that encompasses rest, worship, social justice, and a covenantal relationship with God. It serves as a weekly reminder of freedom from slavery, an act of trust in God's provision, and a rehearsal for a future perfect world.

Understanding Shabbat through Scripture thus invites us into a rhythm of life that is both ancient and strikingly relevant. It challenges us to consider what it means to truly rest, to set aside a sacred time in our increasingly secular world, and to cultivate a practice that nourishes our deepest needs for connection, reflection, and peace.

What did Yeshua teach about keeping the Shabbat?

Yeshua had a distinctive approach to observing the Shabbat, which often set Him apart from the religious leaders of His time. His teachings and actions on this matter provide a fascinating insight into the broader message of His ministry and the transformative nature of His approach to religious observance and law, in particular the Shabbat.

The Shabbat is the seventh day of the week, a day of rest and worship commanded by God to the Israelites as a sign of the covenant. In the time of Yeshua, the Pharisees and other religious leaders had developed a complex set of rules defining what it meant to keep the Sabbath holy. These rules were meant to ensure that no work was done on this day, preserving its sanctity.

Yeshua's teachings on the Sabbath, as recorded in the New Testament, reveal a different focus. He did not dismiss the importance of the Sabbath, but He challenged the rigid legalism with which it was often observed. One of the core principles He emphasised was the Sabbath's purpose: a day made for man's benefit, not man for the Sabbath's sake. This perspective is vividly illustrated in several episodes from the Gospels.

One such incident occurred when Yeshua and His disciples walked through grain fields on the Sabbath. The disciples, hungry, began to pick some heads of grain to eat. This act was deemed by some Pharisees as work, thereby breaking the Sabbath law. Yeshua responded with a reminder of the biblical precedent set by David, who ate the consecrated bread from the temple when in need, highlighting the precedence of human need over ritual compliance. He asserted,

"The Son of Man is Lord even of the Sabbath,"

indicating His authority to define what was lawful on the Sabbath.

Another powerful example of Yeshua's stance on the Sabbath was His healing on this day. On several occasions, He healed the sick during the Sabbath, which sparked controversy among the religious leaders. They considered healing work and thus inappropriate for the Sabbath.

In one instance, when Yeshua healed a man with a withered hand, He confronted the legalistic mindset by asking,

"Is it lawful on the Sabbath to do good or to do evil, to save life or to kill?"

His question exposed the heart of the issue: the well-being of a person is more important than strict rule-following. Through His actions, Yeshua demonstrated that doing good and saving life aligns with the true spirit of the Sabbath.

These actions and teachings of Yeshua highlight a significant difference in perspective. While the religious leaders of the day emphasised strict adherence to a set of rules, Yeshua emphasised the underlying principles of love, mercy, and compassion. Hetaught that the Sabbath was a day to celebrate God's creation and to rest in His provision, not a day to be burdened by excessive regulations that detract from its joy and purpose.

Furthermore, Yeshua's approach to the Sabbath was integrative, not just focusing on what not to do, but also on what should be done. He viewed the Sabbath as an opportunity to reflect on God's goodness, to engage in acts of kindness, and to restore life. This was revolutionary in a context where religious observance was often measured by external adherence to rules rather than the cultivation of an inward spiritual relationship.

Yeshua's approach to the Sabbath and other aspects of religious law often put Him at odds with the religious authorities. His perspective was seen as radical, yet it resonated with many who found the existing religious systems burdensome and exclusive. By prioritising human need and the intention behind the law, Yeshua called people back to the heart of God's commandments.

In contrast to the religious leaders who often used the law to exert power and control, Yeshua used the law to reveal God's love and to guide people into a deeper, more authentic relationship with Him. He sought to remove the barriers that religious legalism had erected, showing that the law's ultimate purpose was to facilitate, not hinder, a genuine relationship with God.

His approach to the Sabbath was not just about legal definitions of work but about the broader context of what it means to live a life dedicated to God. Yeshua's life and teachings demonstrated that the Sabbath, like all divine commandments, was designed to bring freedom, joy, and life to humanity, not to impose unnecessary burdens or restrictions.

The controversies that Yeshua's Sabbath activities sparked are indicative of the broader tensions between His message and the prevailing religious norms. He was often criticised by the religious leaders for His actions, but for many ordinary people, His approach was liberating. It provided a new way of understanding and living out the commandments, one that emphasised the spirit of the law over the letter.

Yeshua's teachings on the Sabbath offer profound insights into His broader religious and ethical message. He emphasised the importance of compassion, mercy, and human need, challenging the prevailing legalistic and rule-bound approach to religious observance.

Through His words and deeds, He demonstrated that the Sabbath was designed to be a blessing to humanity, a day of rest, rejuvenation, and joy, rather than a burden of compliance and restriction. This perspective not only differentiated Him from the religious leaders of His time but also highlighted the transformative nature of His ministry, which sought to bring individuals into a loving and life-giving relationship with God.

How can we follow Yeshua's teaching concerning the keeping of the Shabbat in today's world?

In today's fast-paced modern world, the idea of observing Shabbat, a day of rest, might seem like a quaint relic from a bygone era. However, the teachings of Yeshua about keeping the Shabbat are not only relevant but also potentially life-changing in our hectic lives. Yeshua's perspective on Shabbat can guide us to rediscover the essence of this day and integrate it into our contemporary lifestyle.

Yeshua's approach to Shabbat was revolutionary in its simplicity and depth. He emphasised the spirit rather than the letter of the law, teaching that Shabbat was made for man, not man for the Shabbat. This principle is a game-changer. It means that Shabbat is a gift to us, a day for our benefit, rather than a burden of strict rules to follow.

In practising Shabbat today, we can take this core idea and apply it to our lives. Shabbat can become a day to unplug from the relentless pace of modern life, to rest, and to refocus on what truly matters. It's about taking a step back from our daily grind to breathe, reflect, and connect with others and with the divine.

To start, embracing the spirit of Shabbat means rethinking our relationship with technology, which, while beneficial, often dominates our lives. A "digital detox" on Shabbat can help us break free from the constant distractions of emails, social media, and news alerts. This isn't just about adhering to a religious rule;

it's about reclaiming our time and attention, allowing us to be more present with our loved ones and ourselves.

Moreover, Shabbat can be a time to cultivate gratitude and mindfulness. In his teachings, Yeshua often highlighted the importance of being mindful and thankful for the blessings in our lives. Observing Shabbat can be a practice in mindfulness, where we slow down, savour the moment, and appreciate the simple joys of life, from a shared meal with family to the beauty of nature.

Yeshua also taught about the importance of helping others and doing good deeds. Shabbat can be an opportunity to focus on acts of kindness and community service. Whether it's volunteering, helping a neighbour, or simply being there for a friend, these actions embody the spirit of Shabbat and reflect Yeshua's teachings about love and compassion.

In embracing the true essence of Shabbat as taught by Yeshua, we also find a rhythm of work and rest that is not only sustainable but also enriching. It's about balancing our productivity with periods of rest, ensuring that we don't burn out and that we maintain our physical, mental, and spiritual well-being.

To integrate Shabbat into our modern lives, we can start small. It doesn't have to be an all-or-nothing approach. Maybe it begins with setting aside a few hours of quiet reflection or family time, gradually expanding as we find what works best for us. The key is intentionality - making deliberate choices about how we spend our time on this day.

Following Yeshua's teachings about keeping the Shabbat in today's world is not about rigidly adhering to a set of ancient rules. Instead, it's about rediscovering the gift of rest, reflection, and connection. Shabbat can be a powerful counterbalance to the pressures of modern life, offering us a time to pause, recharge, and focus on what truly matters. By embracing the spirit of Shabbat, we can lead more balanced, fulfilling, and meaningful lives.

Chapter 8.

The Fifth Commandment - The foundations of respect

"Honour your father and your mother, that your days may be long upon the land which the Lord your God is giving you".

What does Scripture tell us about the fifth commandment?

Understanding the fifth commandment,

"Honour your father and your mother, that your days may be long upon the land which the Lord your God is giving you,"

is like peeling an onion; layers of meaning and significance exist to uncover.

This commandment, found in Exodus 20:12 and Deuteronomy 5:16, is a cornerstone of the moral foundation delivered to the Israelites on Mount Sinai. It bridges the commandments that focus on our relationship with God and those that concern our relationships with others. The first layer to consider is the literal meaning of the commandment. To honour your father and mother is to show them respect, obedience, and care. This was a revolutionary idea in the ancient world, where the elderly could be seen as a burden.

In Hebrew, the word for "honour" (kabed) directly translates to "give weight" or "glorify." This suggests a substantial, tangible form of respect, one that involves recognising the significance and worth of one's parents.

Delving deeper, the commandment carries a promise:

"that your days may be long upon the land which the Lord your

God is giving you."

This is one of the few commandments with a stated reward, indicating its importance in the biblical worldview. The promise of longevity is tied to honouring one's parents, suggesting a cause-and-effect relationship in the moral and spiritual economy of the Bible. This promise also connects personal behaviour with collective well-being, insinuating that a society honouring familial bonds will thrive.

Historically, the commandment has been seen as foundational for societal stability. In ancient Israelite society, the family unit was central to social, economic, and religious life. Parents were the primary conveyors of tradition, faith, and identity. By honouring them, individuals maintained family harmony and preserved cultural and religious heritage. This reinforcement of family structures ensured the transmission of values and wisdom from generation to generation.

The commandment also embodies a reciprocal nature of care. While children are commanded to honour their parents, this implies a responsibility for parents to be honourable. They are to nurture, educate, and guide their children, creating a worthy environment for honour. This reciprocal care ensures a balanced family dynamic where respect and love are mutual.

In the broader scriptural context, honouring one's parents is not isolated; it is part of a covenantal relationship between God and His people. The Israelites were chosen to live according to God's law, setting an example for the nations. Thus, the commandment is not merely about familial respect but is also a component of their witness to God's righteousness and love.

The ethical implications of this commandment are profound. It establishes the principle that honouring human relationships is integral to spiritual life. The respect for parental authority symbolises a respect for divine authority.

Just as children are to honour their parents, so too are the people of God expected to honour Him. This mirrors the Ten Commandments' structure, where the first set focuses on the relationship with God and the second on relationships with others.

Theological interpretations often view the commandment as teaching respect for all authority, not just parental. By learning to honour their parents, children develop a respect for community leaders, teachers, and, ultimately, God. This respect for authority creates a respectful society where people can live peacefully and lawfully.

The narrative and legal texts in the Bible provide numerous examples of this commandment in action. Stories of family relationships, both functional and dysfunctional, are used to illustrate the consequences of obeying or disobeying this commandment. For example, the narratives of Abraham, Isaac, and Jacob show the complexities of family life and the importance of maintaining familial bonds.

Moreover, the commandment's significance transcends time and culture, addressing the universal human experience of being part of a family. It speaks to the ongoing need to balance personal autonomy with communal responsibility.

In ancient times, honouring one's parents was also about preserving the family lineage and property. While the societal context may have changed, respecting and caring for one's family remains relevant today.

In interpreting this commandment, early biblical commentators emphasised the spiritual virtues of gratitude and humility. Honouring parents is an act of gratitude for the life and care they have given. It is also an exercise in humility, acknowledging one's origins and dependence. This fosters a spirit of thankfulness and respect, which is essential in the biblical ethical framework.

So, the fifth commandment, "Honour your father and your mother," is rich in meaning and implication. It serves as a cornerstone for individual morality and societal stability, emphasising the importance of family, the virtue of respect, and the interconnectedness of human and divine relationships.

Through its personal, social, and spiritually significant layers, this commandment teaches timeless principles of respect, gratitude, and responsibility, forming a vital link between love for God and others. Its place in the Decalogue underscores the inseparable bond between our reverence for the divine and our actions in the human community, guiding us in pursuing a just and compassionate society.

What did Yeshua teach about the fifth commandment?

Yeshua had a transformative approach to the teachings of the Torah, including the Ten Commandments. Among these ancient laws, the fifth commandment instructs,

"Honour your father and your mother, that your days may be long upon the land which the Lord your God is giving you."

Yeshua's perspective on this commandment was both a reinforcement of its traditional meaning and an expansion of its application, embodying a deeper, more spiritual interpretation.

In Yeshua's time, the commandment to honour one's parents was understood literally, emphasising respect, obedience, and care, particularly in their old age. This was culturally significant in asociety where family lineage and honour were pivotal. However, Yeshua introduced a nuanced understanding that both upheld and transcended the conventional wisdom of his era.

Yeshua's teachings often went to the heart of the law, probing the intentions and attitudes behind actions. He emphasised the spirit of the law over its letter, guiding people to understand the principles of love, respect, and duty represented by the commandments.

When discussing the fifth commandment, Yeshua didn't just speak about honouring parents; he delved into what it means to live a life that genuinely reflects this respect and honour.

He expanded the concept of family, teaching that all people are part of a broader spiritual family under God. In Mark 3:35, He says,

"For whoever does the will of God, he is My brother and sister and mother."

Here, Yeshua elevates the concept of honour to include the family one is born into and the family formed by divine relationship and spiritual kinship.

For Yeshua, honouring one's parents was not just about filial duty but was connected to a larger framework of loving one's neighbour and living righteously. He taught that the true expression of honouring parents was not merely through outward actions but through living a life that embodies the values they have instilled.

Yeshua also critiqued the religious leaders of his time for their hypocrisy, pointing out how some interpreted the law in ways that allowed them to neglect their parents under the guise of religious piety.

In Matthew 15:4-6, He criticises the Pharisees for allowing people to say to their parents,

'Whatever support you might have had from me is Corban'

(corban meaning, devoted to God), nullifying the commandment for the sake of their tradition. Yeshua pointed out that honouring one's parents is not just about financial or verbal support but encompasses a heartfelt recognition of their role in one's life.

Yeshua often used parables, simple stories that illustrate a moral or spiritual lesson in teaching about this commandment. Through these parables, he conveyed the importance of understanding and internalising the commandment's essence.

One such teaching is the parable of the prodigal son, which illustrates forgiveness, acceptance, and unconditional love - key aspects of honouring one's parents.

Yeshua's interpretation of the fifth commandment underscores a principle beyond age, time, or social norms. He highlighted the importance of a heartfelt commitment to family values, showing that honour and respect are fundamental to healthy relationships and communities. His approach was radical for its time, challenging existing norms and calling for a more profound, introspective adherence to God's laws.

Moreover, Yeshua's teachings on honouring parents serve as a lens through which to view our relationships with authority figures and elders. He taught that respect should not be conditional or self-serving but rooted in genuine love and reverence for others. According to Yeshua, this respect reflects one's relationship with God, as honouring one's parents is akin to honouring God, the ultimate parent to all.

Yeshua's teachings on the fifth commandment reveal a rich perspective that honours the traditional Jewish teaching while deepening it to include a broader, more inclusive understanding of family and community.

He taught that to honour one's parents truly is to live a life of love, respect, and integrity, extending these values to all relationships. Through his words and actions, Yeshua demonstrated that honouring one's parents is not just a duty to be fulfilled but a way of life that encompasses the whole being, linking the individual, family, community, and the divine in a harmonious and life-affirming way.

How can we follow Yeshua's teaching about the fifth commandment in the modern world?

The fifth commandment, "Honour your father and mother," as Yeshua taught, has timeless relevance yet poses unique challenges and opportunities in today's world.

This commandment, rooted in ancient wisdom, is straightforward in its directive but more complex in its application, touching family dynamics and broader societal relationships.

First and foremost, honouring parents is about showing them respect, love, and gratitude. It goes beyond mere obedience, especially as we grow older and become independent.

In the contemporary context, this could manifest in various ways, like maintaining regular communication with parents, regardless of the physical distance. With technology at our fingertips, we have no excuse not to call, text, or video chat, keeping the bonds strong and showing that we care.

Financial support is another aspect, especially in societies where elderly care is a personal responsibility. Supporting parents in their old age, ensuring they have what they need to live comfortably, is a practical way of honouring them. It's not just about fulfilling a duty; it's about reciprocating the love and care they provided during our upbringing.

However, honouring parents is not always about agreement or submission, especially in cases where relationships are strained or have become toxic. Sometimes, honouring them means settinghealthy boundaries, ensuring mutual respect and well-being. It's about balancing respect and personal integrity, navigating complex family dynamics with grace and understanding.

Moreover, Yeshua's teaching on honouring parents also opens the door to a broader interpretation: respecting and valuing the older generations.

In many societies, there's a growing disconnect between the young and the old, often leading to isolation and neglect of the elderly. Honouring them involves listening to their stories, learning from their experiences, and valuing their contributions to society, ensuring they feel respected and included.

But can this commandment extend beyond the familial and generational context? Yes, because at its heart, it's about fostering respect, empathy, and kindness in our relationships. In a broader sense, it can apply to how we treat others in our community.

Honouring others could mean respecting those in authority, like teachers, leaders, and mentors, and acknowledging their roles and contributions to our growth and society.

Furthermore, in a world increasingly characterised by diversity and pluralism, honouring each other means respecting different cultures, traditions, and viewpoints. It's about engaging with others with a posture of learning and appreciation, recognising every person's inherent worth and dignity.

In professional settings, this principle can transform workplace dynamics. Treating colleagues respectfully, valuing their ideas and contributions, and fostering a culture of mutual support and recognition aligns with honouring others. It promotes a healthy, productive work environment where everyone feels valued and respected.

In community life, honouring each other means active participation and contribution to the collective well-being. It's about being a good neighbour, a reliable friend, and a committed citizen, involved in local initiatives, and showing care for the community's environment and resources.

However, living out this commandment is not without challenges. Modern life is fast-paced and often individualistic, making it easy to overlook the importance of nurturing relationships and community bonds. It requires intentional effort and commitment to prioritise these values in daily life, to slow down and appreciate the people around us.

Moreover, while offering unprecedented connectivity, the digital age also presents new challenges in how we honour each other. Online interactions can sometimes be impersonal or even disrespectful. Navigating these spaces with the intent to honour and respect others calls for mindfulness and discernment, ensuring our digital footprint reflects the values of kindness and respect.

So, how can we practise this in our daily lives? It starts with small, everyday actions. Listening attentively when someone speaks, showing appreciation and gratitude, offering help without being asked, and being patient and forgiving when conflicts arise. Theseactions, though seemingly insignificant, can have a profound impact on our relationships and communities.

So, honouring your father and mother, as Yeshua taught, is a principle that extends far beyond the family unit, touching every aspect of our lives and relationships. It's a call to live with respect, empathy, and love towards everyone we encounter. By embodying this commandment, we not only enrich our own lives but also contribute to a kinder, more compassionate world.

Chapter 9.

The Sixth Commandment - The Sanctity of Life.

"You shall not murder.

What does Scripture tell us about not committing murder?

The Sixth Commandment, "Do not murder," found in the Book of Exodus 20:13 and Deuteronomy 5:17, is a succinct directive that has echoed through millennia, shaping the moral and ethical frameworks of societies across the globe.

Its brevity belies the depth of its implications and the broad spectrum of interpretations and discussions it has inspired among theologians, philosophers, and legal experts. This chapter delves into what scripture tells us about this commandment, exploring its context, the nuances of its language, and its place within the broader tapestry of biblical law and narrative.

To begin with, the commandment's context within the Ten Commandments is crucial for understanding its significance. TheTen Commandments serve as a foundational ethical code God gave to Moses on Mount Sinai, intended to guide the Israelites in their relationship with God and one another. The Sixth Commandment is part of the second tablet, which deals primarily with interpersonal relationships. This positioning underscores the importance of human life in the community's moral fabric and God's view of life as sacred.

The Hebrew phrase used in the commandment, "לֹא תִרְצָח" (lo tirtzach), is often translated as "do not murder" rather than "do not kill." This distinction is significant. The word "tirtzach" refers specifically to unlawful killing, implying premeditation and intent. This differentiation acknowledges that not all taking of life falls under the prohibition of this commandment. For instance, killing in self-defence or in times of war is not addressed here. The focus is on the sanctity of human life and the prohibition against unjustly taking it away.

Exploring further, the commandment's implications extend beyond the act of murder itself, touching on attitudes and behaviours that devalue human life. Biblical narratives and laws frequently emphasise the importance of treating others with dignity and respect and recognising the image of God in every person.

For instance, the story of Cain and Abel in Genesis 4 illustrates the destructive path of jealousy and anger, leading to the first murder. While predating the giving of the Law, this narrative highlights the themes of responsibility towards others and the consequences of failing to uphold the sanctity of life.

Moreover, the Bible includes several laws that expand on the Sixth Commandment, providing guidance on issues such as manslaughter, revenge, and justice.

For example, the establishment of cities of refuge in Numbers 35 provides a mechanism for protecting those who have killed unintentionally, distinguishing between accidental death and murder. This legal framework emphasises the importance of intention in assessing guilt and the value of providing avenues for redemption and restoration.

The prophetic writings also contribute to our understanding of the Sixth Commandment by linking justice and righteousness with respect for life. Prophets like Isaiah and Micah speak out against violence and exploitation, calling the people to live out the implications of their covenant relationship with God in how they treat one another. These exhortations remind us that adherence to the commandment extends beyond the avoidance of murder to encompass a commitment to social justice and the protection of the vulnerable.

In the wisdom literature, such as Proverbs, we find reflections on how hatred, envy, and strife can lead to violence and destruction. These texts offer practical advice on how to live in harmony with others, highlighting the importance of self-control, kindness, and peacemaking in preventing conflict and preserving life.

Throughout the biblical narrative, the Sixth Commandment serves as a touchstone for discussions about the value of human life and the community's responsibility to protect it. It challenges individuals and societies to reflect on their attitudes towards others and to seek ways to uphold the dignity and sanctity of every person. The commandment's enduring relevance lies in its call to recognize the divine image in our fellow human beings and to commit ourselves to actions that affirm and protect that sacred value.

The Sixth Commandment, "Do not murder," encapsulates a profound respect for human life that permeates scripture. Its implications go far beyond the prohibition of unlawful killing, inviting us to consider the ways in which our actions, attitudes, and societal structures either affirm or undermine the sanctity of life.

By exploring the depths of this commandment, we are challenged to live out the values of justice, mercy, and compassion at the heart of biblical ethics. The commandment is a testament to God's value on human life and serves as a moral compass guiding us towards a more just and compassionate world.

What did Yeshua teach about the sixth commandment?

Yeshua's teachings, particularly on the sixth commandment, "You shall not murder," offer a profound exploration into the essence of moral conduct and the spirit of the law beyond its literal interpretation.

His insights, delivered with remarkable depth yet understandable simplicity, delve into the underpinnings of human behaviour, urging a transformation that transcends the mere act of refraining from physical violence.

In examining His teachings, we uncover a comprehensive ethical framework that challenges individuals to cultivate inner purity, empathy, and a profound respect for life.

Yeshua's discourse on the sixth commandment makes it evident that His teachings are not merely prohibitive but fundamentally transformative. He invites individuals to embark on a journey of self-examination, urging them to confront and rectify the negative emotions and impulses that can lead to the ultimate transgression of taking a life.

His interpretation and expansion of the Mosaic Law's Sixth Commandment, "You shall not murder" (Exodus 20:13; Deuteronomy 5:17), stand out for its depth.

Instead of merely reiterating the commandment's prohibition against taking another's life, Yeshua delved into the commandment's spiritual and ethical implications, emphasising the importance of the intentions and emotions that lead to actions.

Through His teachings, particularly those encapsulated in the Sermon on the Mount (Matthew 5-7), Yeshua reaffirmed the commandment and expanded its scope to include anger, reconciliation, and love for enemies.

Yeshua's approach to the Sixth Commandment can be seen as part of a broader effort to internalise the Law, moving beyond its literal observance to emphasise the purity of heart and intention. In Matthew 5:21-22, Yeshua challenged His followers to examine their actions and the emotions and thoughts that precede actions.

"You have heard that it was said to the people long ago, 'You shall not murder, and anyone who murders will be subject to judgement.' But I tell you that anyone angry with a brother or sister will be subject to judgement."

Here, Yeshua equates anger with murder in moral terms, suggesting that harbouring anger is tantamount to committing murder in one's heart. This radical interpretation underscores the belief that sin begins with inner attitudes and emotions, not external actions.

The call to reconcile with others before offering gifts at the altar (Matthew 5:23-24) further illustrates Yeshua's emphasis on internalising the commandment against murder.

"So if you are offering your gift at the Temple altar and you remember there that your brother has something against you, leave your gift where it is by the altar, go and make peace with your brother. Then come back and offer your gift".

By urging reconciliation, Yeshua teaches that relationships and harmony are paramount, transcending religious rituals. This perspective prioritises the restoration of relationships over adherence to ritual, highlighting the interconnectedness of ethical behaviour and spiritual devotion.

Moreover, Yeshua's directive to love one's enemies and pray for those who persecute you (Matthew 5:43 - 44) expands the Sixth Commandment's implications even further.

"You have heard it said, 'Love your neighbour and hate your enemy.' But I tell you, love your enemies and pray for those who persecute you."

By advocating for love towards enemies, Yeshua challenges the natural inclination towards hatred and retaliation, proposing a radical non-violence that seeks the well-being of all individuals, even those who may wish harm. This teaching not only prohibits physical violence but also condemns hatred, which can be seen as internal murder.

Yeshua's interpretation of the Sixth Commandment is also reflected in his interactions with individuals and groups throughout the Gospels. His approach to those considered sinners, marginalised, or enemies demonstrate a consistent application of the principles of forgiveness, reconciliation, and love.

For example, his willingness to forgive and show compassion, even to those who betrayed or denied Him, exemplifies the living embodiment of His teachings on the commandments.

The emphasis on the heart's condition is a recurring theme in Yeshua's teachings. He consistently taught that outward compliance with the law is insufficient without inner transformation. This perspective is encapsulated in the notion that what defiles a person comes from the heart (Mark 7:20-23), further reinforcing the idea that sin, including murder, begins with inner attitudes and intentions.

He continued, "What comes out of a man is what makes a man unclean. In fact, from within, out of people's hearts, come evil thoughts, sexual sins, theft, murder, adultery, greed, wickedness, deceit, unrestrained immorality, envy, slander, arrogance, and foolishness. All these evil things proceed from within and it is that which makes a person unclean."

Yeshua's expansion of the Sixth Commandment has profound implications for understanding the nature of sin, ethics, and the path to spiritual fulfilment. By focusing on the root causes of actions, such as anger and hatred, Yeshua calls for a comprehensive transformation of the individual's heart and mind. This transformation involves refraining from physical acts of violence and cultivating attitudes of love, forgiveness, and reconciliation.

Yeshua's teachings on the Sixth Commandment, "You shall not murder," go far beyond a simple prohibition against taking life. They represent a profound and comprehensive ethical framework that addresses the roots of violence in human emotions and thoughts.

Through His emphasis on internal transformation, reconciliation, and love, Yeshua challenges individuals to live in a way that transcends legalistic adherence to commandments, aiming instead for a transformation of the heart that reflects the essence of divine law. This approach not only deepens the understanding of the commandment itself but also offers a vision of a more compassionate and harmonious way of living, rooted in the values of forgiveness, love, and respect for all life.

How can we follow Yeshua's teaching on the sixth commandment in the modern world?

In today's fast-paced, technologically advanced, and often polarised world, the teachings of Yeshua, especially regarding the sixth commandment, "You shall not murder," hold profound significance and present both challenges and opportunities for application.

At its core, this commandment underscores the sanctity of human life, emphasising that every individual is of immeasurable value and deserving of respect and protection.

Yet, to embody this teaching in the modern context requires more than merely abstaining from physical violence. It involves a deep commitment to nurturing life, fostering understanding, promoting peace, and cultivating a community where every person can thrive.

Understanding the essence of "You shall not murder" in the

contemporary era extends beyond the literal interpretation of refraining from taking another's life. It encompasses a broader, more inclusive approach to supporting and sustaining life in all its forms.

This interpretation invites us to consider how our actions, words, and even thoughts can either affirm or negate the value of life. Therefore, following Yeshua's teaching today involves an effort towards both personal and collective transformation. At the personal level, adhering to this commandment means cultivating an attitude of respect and love towards oneself and others. It involves recognizing the intrinsic worth of every individual, regardless of their background, beliefs, or lifestyle.

This respect for life compels us to act with compassion and kindness, to speak words that uplift rather than tear down, and to resolve conflicts peacefully without resorting to harm. In a world where anger, resentment, and division often lead to violence, both physical and verbal, choosing to respond with understanding and empathy is a powerful testament to the value we place on life.

Moreover, following Yeshua's teaching requires us to be mindful of how our lifestyles and choices impact others and the world around us. In an age where consumerism and indifference can lead to exploitation and suffering, making ethical choices that promote the well-being of others, including advocating for fair trade, supporting sustainable practices, and opposing systems that perpetuate injustice, is essential.

This aspect of living out the commandment underscores the interconnectedness of all life and our responsibility to act in ways that preserve and enhance life, not only for our immediate circle but for the global community.

At a communal level, embodying the principle of "You shall not murder" means actively participating in efforts that promote peace, justice, and the sanctity of life. It involves working towards ending violence in all its forms, including war, terrorism, domestic abuse, and systemic injustices that degrade human dignity.

Engaging in or supporting initiatives that aim to address the root causes of violence, such as poverty, inequality, and lack of education, reflects a commitment to upholding the sanctity of life. Additionally, advocating for policies and practices that protect the vulnerable, provide for the needy, and ensure justice for all demonstrates a collective adherence to this commandment.

Furthermore, in the digital age, where online interactions can often dehumanise and lead to cyberbullying, harassment, and spreading hate, following Yeshua's teaching calls for a conscious effort to promote kindness, understanding, and respect in our virtual engagements.

The anonymity and distance the internet provides should not be an excuse to harm others with our words or actions. Instead, it presents an opportunity to extend the principles of love and respect for life into new realms, fostering communities that are supportive and life-affirming, even in the digital world.

Education and dialogue also play crucial roles in living out the commandment "You shall not murder" today. By fostering a culture that values critical thinking, empathy, and mutual respect, we can challenge the prejudices, stereotypes, and misinformation that often lead to animosity and violence. Creating spaces for open, honest conversations about difficult issues, including racial, religious, and cultural differences, can help break down barriers and build bridges of understanding and peace.

Following Yeshua's teaching on this commandment involves personal and communal introspection and repentance for the ways in which we may have consciously or unconsciously contributed to the culture of violence and disregard for life.

Acknowledging our shortcomings and seeking to change our attitudes and actions is a vital step towards embodying the fullness of this commandment. It is through this process of continual learning, growth, and transformation that we can truly honour the sanctity of life in our thoughts, words, and deeds.

Adhering to Yeshua's teaching on the sixth commandment, "You shall not murder," in the modern world, is a comprehensive endeavour that touches every aspect of our lives. It challenges us to see beyond the literal prohibition of killing to a broader, more profound commitment to promoting and protecting life in all its forms.

By cultivating respect and love for ourselves and others, making ethical choices, participating in efforts to promote peace and justice, fostering kindness in digital spaces, engaging in meaningful education and dialogue, and committing to personal and communal growth, we can live out this commandment in a way that reflects its true spirit and relevance for our time.

Through these actions, we not only honour the sanctity of life but also contribute to the creation of a world where every person can experience the fullness of life that Yeshua's teachings aspire to offer.

Chapter 10.

The Seventh Commandment - Fidelity and Trust.

"You shall not commit adultery".

What does Scripture tell us about the seventh commandment - "You shall not commit adultery?"

The seventh commandment, "You shall not commit adultery," stands as a pivotal directive within the Torah, specifically articulated in Exodus 20:14 and Deuteronomy 5:18. This commandment, part of the Ten Commandments received by Moses on Mount Sinai, serves as a foundational element of moral and ethical guidance in the Judeo-Christian tradition. At its essence, the commandment promotes fidelity, trust, and the sanctity of the marital bond, underpinning the moral and spiritual framework that guides believers in their personal and communal lives.

Adultery, in its most basic definition, involves a married individual engaging in sexual relations with someone other than their spouse. However, the implications of this act, as delineated in scriptural texts, are far-reaching, touching upon loyalty, community integrity, and personal integrity.

Historically, marriage was viewed not merely as a personal agreement but as a covenant encompassing social, economic, and spiritual dimensions. Thus, an act of adultery was perceived not only as a personal failing but as an affront to societal order and divine statute.

The gravity of adultery is underscored within the Old Testament, where the commandment is interwoven with narratives that explore relationships, community standards, and divine expectations.

For example, Leviticus 20:10 prescribes death for both individuals involved in adultery, highlighting the act's seriousness to the community and God.

If a man has sexual relations with his neighbour's wife, both the man and the woman are guilty of adultery and must be put to death!

This severe penalty reflects the understanding of the marital relationship as sacred and inviolable, intended to mirror the faithfulness and commitment seen in the covenant between God and His people.

The prohibition of adultery also relates to the concept of property and the patriarchal structure of ancient societies, where a wife was viewed as her husband's property. Such a perspective, while outdated and rejected in modern discussions on marriage, played a crucial role in historical understandings of marital fidelity and the consequences of adultery.

The narrative of King David and Bathsheba, detailed in 2 Samuel 11, serves as a poignant scriptural case study on the ramifications of adultery. David, despite being a man "after God's own heart," falls into the sin of adultery with Bathsheba, leading to deceit, the arranged death of her husband Uriah, and divine displeasure.

This story highlights the cascading effects of sin, starting with adultery but leading to a series of increasingly grave offences. Nathan the prophet's confrontation of David (2 Samuel 12) and the subsequent divine punishment point to the serious consequences of violating the seventh commandment, not only for the individuals directly involved but for their community and relationship with God.

The wisdom literature of the Old Testament, particularly in Proverbs, further reflects on adultery's moral implications. For instance, Proverbs 6:32 frames adultery as an act of profound personal folly leading to self-destruction.

But a man who commits adultery is a fool. He brings about his own destruction.

This perspective highlights the act's far-reaching consequences, affecting one's social standing, family relationships, and personal integrity.

Adultery, within the broader biblical narrative, underscores the value of loyalty, trust, and faithfulness - qualities essential to the covenantal relationship between God and His people. The prophets frequently use adultery as a metaphor for Israel's unfaithfulness to God, illustrating the broader theme of betrayal of a covenant, whether marital or spiritual.

Exploring the roots of the commandment against adultery, Scripture emphasises the sanctity of marriage, established in the early pages of Genesis as a covenant relationship ordained by God. This divine intention for marriage frames the understanding of adultery as a violation of both the spouse and divine will.

The personal and communal havoc illustrated by the story of David and Bathsheba, along with reflections in Proverbs on the self-destructive nature of adultery, highlight the broader societal ethos that the commandment seeks to cultivate.

Furthermore, Scripture addresses the condition of the heart, calling for purity and integrity beyond mere compliance with the law. This deeper examination reflects a call to cultivate a character marked by loyalty, integrity, and love, principles that guide not only personal behaviour but also the moral fabric of society.

The commandment against adultery transcends a prohibition against a specific act, embodying a call to honour the sanctity of marriage, live with integrity, and maintain a pure heart. Through various narratives and teachings, Scripture presents a comprehensive view of the devastation wrought by adultery and calls for a higher standard of living that respects covenantal bonds and reflects the character of a holy and faithful God.

This commandment, therefore, not only safeguards the well-being of families and societies but also invites individuals into a deeper, more faithful relationship with the Creator, emphasising the interconnectedness of personal choices, community standards, and spiritual commitments.

What did Yeshua teach about the seventh commandment - You shall not commit adultery?

In the heart of the biblical narrative, the book of Exodus 20:14 delivers a clear directive: "You shall not commit adultery." Originally presented to the Israelites, this command forms a cornerstone of a broader covenant with God, aiming to establish high moral standards for individual behaviour and the ethical foundation of the community.

Yet, the New Testament introduces a profound expansion of this commandment through the teachings of Yeshua, who places a significant emphasis on the inner condition of the heart rather than solely on outward actions.

During the Sermon on the Mount, a pivotal moment captured in the Gospel of Matthew, Yeshua revisits this commandment, offering a revolutionary reinterpretation that extends its implications far beyond the physical act of adultery.

"You have heard that it was said, 'You shall not commit adultery.' But I tell you that anyone who looks at a woman lustfully has already committed adultery with her in his heart,"

His words, recorded in Matthew 5:27-28, shift the focus to the realm of thought and intention. This teaching redefines what constitutes adultery and underscores the significance of mental and emotional loyalty in relationships, advocating for purity that encompasses both thought and action.

Yeshua consistently emphasises that mere compliance with the law's letter is not enough if the heart remains distant from God's will.

This perspective echoes the broader critique of superficial piety exemplified by the Pharisees and underscores a deeper concern with the inner moral and spiritual state.

The principle that true obedience to God involves aligning one's heart with divine intentions resonates throughout His teachings and finds precedence in the Hebrew Scriptures, such as the wisdom literature of Proverbs, which cautions against the snares of infidelity and underscores the importance of guarding one's heart (Proverbs 6:25-29).

Don't let your heart lust after her beauty or allow her glance to captivate you. The price of a whore is a loaf of bread, but the adulteress is hunting for a precious life. Can a man carry fire inside his shirt without burning his clothes? Can a man walk [barefoot] on hot coals without scorching his feet? So is he who has sex with his neighbour's wife; anyone touching her will be punished.

The Scriptural narrative on adultery does not shy away from discussing its severe consequences. In the Old Testament, adultery is depicted as a grievous offence, warranting strict penalties (Leviticus 20:10).

"If a man has sexual relations with his neighbour's wife, both the man and the woman are guilty of adultery and must be put to death."

While Yeshua's teachings in the New Testament, particularly in Matthew 5, do not delve into these penalties, they profoundly highlight the spiritual consequences of lustful intent, suggesting that harbouring such thoughts can spiritually estrange individuals from God, much like how physical acts of adultery can erode relationships and community cohesion.

By broadening the definition of adultery to encompass lustful thoughts, Yeshua challenges believers to transcend the superficial adherence to the law and embrace a holistic purity that includes both heart and action.

This approach calls for introspection and transformation, urging individuals to align their hearts and minds with divine will. His teachings offer insight into the complexities of human nature and sin, guiding followers towards spiritual integrity through acknowledgment of personal shortcomings and embracing God's forgiveness.

The emphasis on inner purity, intent, and the redemptive power of God's love presents a comprehensive framework for living out the commandment against adultery in a manner that respects the sanctity of relationships and honours the divine.

A memorable instance in Yeshua's ministry, which people often use concerning the law on adultery, is found in John 8:3-11, where Yeshua encounters a woman accused of committing adultery. The law demands that anyone caught in adultery was to be stoned to death.

However, Yeshua's response shows this episode is not a commentary on adultery.

According to the law, both parties caught in adultery were to be judged and punished by stoning them to death, as the quote from Leviticus 10:20 shows. It's inconceivable that those men, renowned for their knowledge of and strict adherence to the law, and who claimed to have caught her in the act, would have ignored the man's involvement and let him go, bringing only the woman for judgement.

Yeshua recognised that his accusers were laying a trap by failing to bring both parties to him, hoping he would wrongly enforce the law's harsh sentence. Yeshua ingeniously used their understanding of the law against them. He challenged them with the statement,

"Whoever is without sin, let him cast the first stone."

The law required that the witnesses to the adultery throw the first stone, but doing so under these circumstances would mean that if they did, they would be bearing false witness - a sin punishable with the same penalty. Thus, he presented them with a stark choice: persist in the falsehood and face the consequences, or abandon their scheme.

So, this episode is clearly about the accusers bearing false witness, not about the woman accused of committing adultery.

Yeshua continued by saying to the woman that he didn't condemn her. But there was nothing to condemn her for regarding the charges these men had brought against her. Forgiveness only comes through repentance, and this woman had nothing to repent of regarding the false charge, so Yeshua never condemned her for that sin. However, he did warn her to stop sinning in all its forms, a warning for all of us.

How can we follow Yeshua's teaching about the seventh commandment - You shall not commit adultery - in the modern world?

The seventh commandment, "You shall not commit adultery," resonates through time, carrying a message that is as relevant today as it was millennia ago. In an era characterised by rapidly changing social norms and the proliferation of digital platforms, adhering to this ancient precept poses unique challenges and opportunities.

So, let's explore how we can live by Yeshua's teachings on this commandment in the contemporary world, focusing on the values of fidelity, integrity, respect, and love.

As we have already discovered, Yeshua's interpretation of the commandments often went beyond their literal meaning, seeking to capture their essence and apply it to the hearts and minds of his followers.

When it comes to adultery, this involves not only the act itself but also the intentions and thoughts that lead to such actions. In Matthew 5:28, Yeshua expands the understanding of adultery, stating,

"But I tell you that anyone who looks at a woman lustfully has already committed adultery with her in his heart."

This profound statement underlines the importance of not just our actions but also our thoughts and intentions.

In today's world, where images and temptations are just a click away, maintaining purity of thought is undoubtedly challenging. The internet, social media, and various forms of entertainment often blur the lines between harmless fun and harmful intentions.

To follow Yeshua's teachings on the seventh commandment, we must develop a mindset that respects others as whole persons, not objects of desire. This respect extends beyond our actions to our thoughts and the digital footprints we leave.

Fidelity, the cornerstone of adhering to the seventh commandment, is about more than avoiding physical acts of infidelity. It encompasses emotional loyalty, intellectual respect, and spiritual unity.

In the modern context, this means being transparent with our partners, sharing our struggles, and seeking help when we find ourselves drawn away from our commitments. It involves setting boundaries around our relationships and digital interactions to safeguard the sanctity of our primary relationships.

Integrity plays a crucial role in following Yeshua's teachings on adultery. In a world where secret lives and alternate personas can be easily maintained online, integrity calls us to be the same person in private that we are in public.

This means our words, actions, and internet clicks should align with our values and commitments. When faced with temptation, we should ask ourselves whether our actions would change if our loved ones were watching.

Living with integrity also involves avoiding situations that could lead to compromise, such as inappropriate conversations or relationships that edge too close to emotional affairs.

Respect is another vital component in adhering to the seventh commandment in today's world. This respect is twofold: respect for oneself and respect for others. By valuing ourselves, recognizing our worth, and understanding our vulnerabilities, we can better navigate the complexities of modern relationships.

Similarly, respecting others means acknowledging their worth, dignity, and boundaries. It means engaging with them deeply, beyond surface-level attractions, and honouring their commitments and ours.

Love, in the context of Yeshua's teachings, is about seeking the best for others. In relationships, this means prioritising our partner's wellbeing, happiness, and growth. True love is patient, kind, and selfless, traits that fortify relationships against the temptations of adultery. It involves daily choices to act in love, even when emotions wane, and to reinvest in our relationships continuously. Practising this kind of love helps create a strong, enduring bond that reflects Yeshua's love for us.

To follow Yeshua's teachings on the seventh commandment in the modern world, we also need to cultivate a supportive community. This involves surrounding ourselves with people who share our values and are committed to helping us uphold them.

Such a community can provide accountability, encouragement, and wisdom when we face challenges. It can also offer perspectives and advice that help us grow in our relationships and maintain our commitments.

Moreover, in our digital age, it's essential to use technology wisely. This includes being discerning about the content we consume, the interactions we engage in online, and the amount of time we spend on digital platforms.

We can set filters, use accountability software, and follow content creators who uplift and encourage healthy relationships. By consciously choosing how we interact with technology, we can reduce the temptations and distractions that might lead us away from our commitments.

Following Yeshua's teachings on the seventh commandment in today's world involves a holistic approach that encompasses our actions, thoughts, and the digital environment we navigate. It requires fidelity, integrity, respect, and love, all of which are grounded in a deep commitment to our relationships and a desire to honour God.

By cultivating these values, surrounding ourselves with a supportive community, and using technology wisely, we can uphold the sacredness of our commitments and reflect Yeshua's teachings in our lives. Through these efforts, we not only avoid adultery but also build stronger, more loving relationships that can withstand the challenges of the modern world.

Chapter 11.

The Eighth Commandment - Integrity in possessions

"You shall not steal.

What does Scripture tell us about the eighth commandment, 'You shall not steal?'

The Eighth Commandment, "You shall not steal," found in Exodus 20:15, embodies a fundamental tenet central to the fabric of ethical, moral, and societal norms across civilisations and cultures throughout history.

This commandment, succinct in its delivery, unveils a profound significance that echoes across time, emphasising the quintessential principle of respecting the property rights of others. It is a clear denunciation of theft, extending its influence beyond mere prohibition to lay the foundation for a culture characterised by trust, mutual respect, and dignity among individuals.

At its core, the Eighth Commandment propels behaviour toward moral integrity and ethical conduct. It recognises and values the complex and hard work individuals put into their labour and subsequent fruits, advocating for safeguarding both personal and communal property.

This advocacy nurtures an environment ripe for trust to thrive - trust between individuals, within communities, and towards societal institutions. Such trust is indispensable for the harmonious coexistence of members within any community.

The Bible offers extensive commentary on the gravity of theft and its repercussions, particularly within the Pentateuch - the first five books that include Exodus. These scriptures delineate the consequences of theft and discuss necessary restitution and the broader socio-economic ramifications of such actions. This comprehensive exploration highlights theft as a transgression with both personal and communal dimensions.

A hallmark of the biblical approach to addressing theft is its emphasis on restorative justice. For instance, the detailed mandates in Exodus 22 and Leviticus 6 for compensating theft victims illustrate a system that extends beyond mere reimbursement. It encompasses apologies, confessions, and, occasionally, additional penalties aimed at righting the wrongs and mending broken relationships. These mandates underscore the importance of admitting one's wrongdoings and actively seeking to make amends.

Furthermore, the Bible demonstrates a keen understanding of the circumstances that may compel individuals to steal, particularly underscoring the roles of poverty and inequality. Scriptures like Proverbs 30:8-9

Keep worthless speech and lies far from me. Do not give me poverty nor riches. Give me food in the amount that is right for me. Too much, and I may feel satisfied, deny you, and say, "Who is the Lord?" Too little, and I may become poor, steal, and profane the name of my God.

and other prophetic utterances call for a society that addresses these underlying causes of theft by aiming to eradicate extreme need. The prophets, in particular, intertwine the battle against theft with the larger struggle for social justice, criticising conditions that push some towards theft as a means of survival.

The Eighth Commandment's message extends beyond a mere prohibition; it envisions a society anchored in fairness, accountability, and collective well-being.

The biblical teachings on theft champion a justice system that punishes wrongdoings, confronts underlying injustices, repairs relationships, and nurtures a community where dignity and rights are universally upheld.

This commandment emphasises the importance of respecting others' possessions and positions the community as a custodian of ethical standards. It advocates avoiding theft and fostering a society built on respect, fairness, and mutual care.

Moreover, it examines the connection between stealing and lying, revealing how theft erodes the fabric of communal trust and coexistence. The focus on restitution and making amends is pivotal, mirroring a deep-seated sense of justice aimed at healing both the victim and the offender.

While the Eighth Commandment specifically forbids theft, its implications reverberate through numerous biblical narratives and teachings.

For example, the story of Zacchaeus in the New Testament, though not directly tied to the commandment, showcases the transformative power of repentance and restitution. Zacchaeus' encounter with Yeshua led him to pledge half of his possessions to the poor and to restore fourfold to anyone he had defrauded (Luke 19:8).

Zacchaeus stood up and said to the Lord, "Lord, I am going to give half of my possessions to the poor. And if I have cheated anyone out of anything, I will pay back four times as much."

This narrative vividly exemplifies the profound impact of acknowledging one's transgressions and actively working towards reconciliation and healing.

In essence, the Eighth Commandment, with its straightforward injunction against theft, intricately interweaves ethical, moral, and spiritual dimensions, guiding us towards a life marked by integrity and a deep respect for the property of others.

By incorporating restitution principles and addressing the roots of theft, the Bible presents a holistic view of justice that encompasses compensating those harmed, facilitating the transformation of wrongdoers, and mending communal ties.

Thus, this timeless commandment transcends the mere prohibition of an act, inviting us to reflect on our actions and their impacts on others and aspiring for a world where respect for individual rights and properties is a universally shared value.

What did Yeshua teach about the eighth commandment, You shall not steal?

Looking at Yeshua's teachings on the eighth commandment, "You shall not steal," necessitates a deeper look into His teachings, parables, and the broader context of His views on ownership, ethics, and morality, as presented in the Gospels of the New Testament.

Though the Gospels do not record Yeshua explicitly discussing the eighth commandment in isolation, His teachings implicitly cover the moral grounds for the principle of not stealing. Examining His teachings can help us derive insights into His stance on honesty, respect for others possessions, and the broader implications of stealing for individual character and society.

In His earthly ministry, Yeshua emphasised the importance of love, compassion, and ethical living as foundational principles of God's kingdom. He taught that adhering to God's commandments was about following rules and transforming the heart and mind to reflect God's righteousness. His approach to the commandments often went beyond their literal interpretation, urging a more profound, spiritual adherence that touches on the essence of moral and ethical living.

In the Sermon on the Mount, Yeshua expounded on the law, moving beyond its literal application to its spiritual and ethical implications. While He didn't explicitly mention the eighth commandment in this sermon, His teachings on material possessions, generosity, and trust in God suggest a framework where stealing becomes a legal wrong and a moral failure to trust in God's provision.

He said, "Do not store up for yourselves treasures on earth, where moths and vermin destroy, and where thieves break in and steal. But store up for yourselves treasures in heaven, where moths and vermin do not destroy, and where thieves do not break in and steal. For where your treasure is, there your heart will be also"

Matthew 6:19-21.

This teaching encourages believers to prioritise spiritual wealth over material wealth, implying that stealing manifests misplaced values and a lack of faith in God's provision.

Yeshua also directly addressed issues related to possessions and wealth through His parables. For instance, the Parable of the Unjust Steward (Luke 16:1-13) criticises dishonesty in managing others' possessions, highlighting the importance of faithfulness and honesty in all dealings. While the parable primarily focuses on the steward's shrewdness, it also underscores the moral expectation that one should not misappropriate what belongs to another, resonating with the commandment's injunction against stealing.

Another significant aspect of Yeshua's teachings related to the eighth commandment is His emphasis on generosity and sharing with the less fortunate. In the story of the rich young ruler (Mark

10:17-27), Yeshua instructed the wealthy man to sell all he had and give to the poor if he wanted to inherit eternal life. This interaction illustrates Yeshua's call to radical generosity and detachment from material possessions, implying that wealth accumulation should not be at the expense of others' well-being, nor should it lead to greed or dishonesty - both of which are closely linked to the act of stealing.

Furthermore, Yeshua's teachings on love and neighbourliness, encapsulated in the Great Commandment - to love God with all one's heart and to love one's neighbour as oneself (Matthew 22:37-40) - implicitly condemn stealing. To love one's neighbour involves respecting their rights and possessions, treating them with the same regard one would have for one's belongings. This principle is the antithesis of stealing, which disregards the rights and well-being of others for personal gain.

Additionally, Yeshua's interaction with Zacchaeus, the tax collector, in Luke 19:1-10 offers a direct glimpse into His response to the act of stealing. Zacchaeus, who had enriched himself at others' expense, was moved by Yeshua's message to repent and restore those he had defrauded fourfold. Yeshua's acceptance of Zacchaeus' repentance and restitution underscores the possibility of redemption and the importance of making amends, aligning with the broader biblical teachings against stealing and emphasising restoration and justice.

So, while Yeshua may not have explicitly discussed the eighth commandment, "You shall not steal," in isolation, His teachings and actions provide a comprehensive moral framework that encompasses and extends the commandment's principles.

Through His emphasis on love, generosity, honesty, and trust in God, Yeshua taught that faithful adherence to God's commandments involves a transformation of the heart that naturally leads to ethical living, where the rights and well-being of others are respected.

His life and teachings call believers to a higher standard of conduct that not only refrains from stealing but actively promotes the flourishing of all individuals in a community rooted in love and mutual respect.

How can we follow Yeshua's teaching about the eighth commandment not to steal in the modern world?

The eighth commandment, "You shall not steal," is a directive that transcends its simple wording to embody a comprehensive ethical principle with profound implications for modern life.

This commandment is not just a rule against theft but a fundamental call to live with integrity, respect for others, and a sense of duty towards the community.

In our contemporary world, characterised by complex social dynamics, rapid technological advancements, and global interconnections, the commandment beckons us to maintain its core values in all aspects of life, from intimate personal interactions to broad societal engagements.

At its heart, the commandment "You shall not steal" underscores the importance of trust and respect in human relationships. It acknowledges every individual's right to the security of their possessions and the fruits of their labour, free from the threat of unwarranted seizure. This principle, simple in its essence, has expansive implications, urging a commitment to honesty, fairness, and empathy in our interactions with one another.

Whether we are navigating the intricacies of personal relationships, conducting business, or engaging in the digital realm, the fundamental principle of not stealing serves as a moral compass, guiding us towards ethical conduct.

In the realm of personal relationships, adherence to this commandment involves a deep respect for the boundaries and possessions of others. This includes carefully considering their privacy and information, which is especially significant in an era where the boundaries between physical and virtual spaces are increasingly blurred. Modern transgressions of this commandment, such as unauthorised sharing of personal information or accessing someone's private digital spaces without consent, highlight the evolving challenges of maintaining integrity in the digital age.

In business and economic activities, the commandment against theft broadens to include ethical practices like fair trade, transparency in transactions, and environmental stewardship. It encourages a rejection of corrupt practices, a commitment to fair labour standards, respect for intellectual property rights, and a conscientious approach to the environmental impacts of our actions.

Recognizing that exploiting natural resources irresponsibly constitutes a form of theft from future generations, this teaching urges us to consider the long-term consequences of our economic behaviours.

The digital domain presents unique ethical challenges, where actions like copyright infringement, often misconceived as victimless crimes, violate the rights and disrespect the efforts of content creators.

The anonymity afforded by the internet can sometimes lead us to overlook the real-world impact of actions such as cyber theft and identity fraud. Upholding the eighth commandment in this context means cultivating a culture of integrity online, protecting personal data, and spreading awareness about the importance of cybersecurity.

At a societal level, the commandment drives us to confront systemic injustices and strive for a world where equitable access to resources is a reality for all. It calls for an understanding of poverty and desperation as drivers of theft, prompting us to advocate for policies and practices that foster equality and social justice.

Moreover, the commandment's relevance extends to the realm of ideas and creativity, underscoring the importance of respecting intellectual property and encouraging a culture of originality and fairness in the creation and sharing of knowledge and artistic works. In an age rich with information, the theft of creative output not only undermines the value of innovation but also diminishes the collective wealth of human creativity.

Yeshua's teachings challenge us to reconsider our relationship with material possessions, urging a focus on spiritual and relational richness over material accumulation. This perspective invites a critical examination of consumerist tendencies, advocating for ethical consumption practices that consider the impact of our purchases on the welfare of others and the health of our planet.

Living by the commandment "You shall not steal" in today's world is an invitation to embody a spirit of generosity, integrity, and justice. It's about respecting the rights and dignity of others, advocating for fairness, protecting the vulnerable, and valuing community and relationships above material gain.

By embracing the essence of this commandment, we lay a foundation for a society built on trust, respect, and mutual care, aligning with the vision of life that Yeshua taught. As we navigate the complexities of contemporary existence, this ancient commandment serves as a crucial guide, challenging us to apply its timeless wisdom to the multifaceted challenges of modern life.

Whether it's respecting intellectual property, fighting against identity theft, living sustainably, or advocating for social justice, the commandment against theft has grown to encompass a wide range of ethical dimensions in our increasingly interconnected world. Committing to live by this commandment means embracing a holistic approach that honours the dignity and rights of others, fostering a world marked by fairness, justice, and shared responsibility for the well-being of our global community.

This comprehensive interpretation not only remains true to the commandment's traditional essence but also expands its application, guiding us toward a more ethical, respectful, and interconnected existence.

Chapter 12.

The Ninth Commandment - A community of justice and honesty.

"You shall not bear false witness against your neighbour.

What does Scripture tell us about the ninth commandment not to bear false witness against your neighbour?

The Ninth Commandment, "You shall not bear false witness against your neighbour," represents a central pillar within the ethical and moral teachings of the Old Testament. This commandment, while on the surface addressing the specific act of lying in a judicial context, extends its reach far beyond to encompass a broad spectrum of actions and behaviours that pertain to honesty, integrity, and the maintenance of trust within a community. Its roots in Scripture are deep and its implications vast, affecting not only personal interactions but also the foundational aspects of societal justice and harmony.

At its heart, the commandment emphasises the sanctity of truth as a divine attribute and its critical role in human relations. The OldTestament is replete with passages that underscore the importance of truthfulness and the dangers of deceit. In Leviticus 19:11, the instruction is clear:

"You shall not steal; you shall not deal falsely; you shall not lie to one another."

This passage reinforces the commandment by explicitly forbidding dishonest behaviours, highlighting the value placed on truth in every aspect of life.

The broader implications of bearing false witness are further elaborated upon in Exodus 23:1-2, where it is written,

"You shall not spread a false report. You shall not join hands with the wicked to act as a malicious witness."

This passage extends the scope of the commandment beyond personal integrity to encompass the responsibility individuals have towards the justice system and their community. It warns against the dangers of contributing to or condoning dishonesty, showcasing the detrimental impact falsehood can have on societal justice and order.

The Ninth Commandment's focus on the protection of a neighbour's reputation, dignity, and well-being through truthfulness reflects a profound understanding of the interconnectedness of human society. In the wisdom literature of the Old Testament, this theme is echoed and expanded. Proverbs 19:5 states,

"A false witness will not go unpunished, and he who breathes out lies will not escape."

This proverb not only affirms the divine disdain for falsehood but also emphasises the inevitable consequences of deceitful actions, reinforcing the societal imperative to uphold truth.

The commitment to truth is seen as a reflection of God's character, as God is consistently depicted as the embodiment of truth in the Scriptures.

Psalm 31:5 refers to God as the *"God of truth,"* while Psalm 117:2 lauds His *"truthful word."*

These references serve to establish a divine benchmark for honesty and integrity, encouraging believers to mirror this divine attribute in their own lives.

The societal ramifications of adhering to or deviating from this commandment are profound. The Old Testament presents a clear depiction of the chaos and injustice that ensue from falsehood, as seen in the story of Achan in Joshua 7, where deceit led to communal suffering and divine displeasure.

Conversely, the story of Joseph in Genesis, who despite facing numerous injustices, maintained his integrity and honesty, exemplifies the blessings and restoration that can come from a commitment to truth.

Moreover, the Ninth Commandment underlines the moral courage required to stand for truth, even in the face of personal risk. This is exemplified in the story of the midwives in Exodus 1, who defied Pharaoh's orders out of their reverence for God's principles of life and truth, showcasing the commandment's call to protect and preserve the well-being of others through acts of truthfulness and courage.

In essence, the Ninth Commandment invites individuals to weave truthfulness into the fabric of their daily lives, fostering relationships and communities characterised by trust, integrity, and justice.

By committing to live in accordance with this command, believers are not only adhering to a biblical mandate but are also contributing to the creation of a world where truth prevails, justice is upheld, and peace and well-being are accessible to all. This commitment to truth, as outlined in the Ninth Commandment, stands as a testament to the enduring relevance and transformative power of these ancient teachings in shaping a just and moral society.

What did Yeshua teach about keeping the ninth commandment not to bear false witness against your neighbour?

Yeshua addressed His time's moral and spiritual landscape with teachings that extended far beyond the letter of the law to its spirit and intended impact on the human heart. Among these teachings, His insights on the Ninth Commandment, *"You shall not bear false witness against your neighbour,"* reveal depths that challenge not just the actions but the inner motivations of individuals.

To understand Yeshua's teaching on this commandment, we must delve into the broader context of His approach to the law as presented in the Hebrew Scriptures. Yeshua did not come to abolish the law but to fulfil it, bringing out its full meaning and showing how its principles apply to the thoughts and attitudes of the heart, not just external actions

"Do not think I came to destroy the Law or the Prophets. I did not come to destroy them but to fulfil them. I tell you: Until heaven and earth pass away, not even the smallest letter, or even part of a letter, will in any way pass away from the Law until everything is fulfilled. So whoever breaks one of the least of these commandments and teaches others to do the same will be called the least in the kingdom of heaven. But whoever practises and teaches them will be called great in the kingdom of heaven. Indeed, I tell you that unless your righteousness surpasses that of the Pharisees and experts in the law, you will never enter the kingdom of heaven.

Matthew 5:17-20.

This perspective is crucial when considering His stance on bearing false witness. Bearing false witness, in its most direct form, refers to lying or misrepresenting the truth about one's neighbour, especially in legal contexts where such falsehoods could lead to unjust outcomes.

However, Yeshua's teachings suggest that this commandment encompasses much more than lies told in court; it includes all forms of deceit, hypocrisy, and actions that mislead or harm others.

In Matthew 5:33-37, Yeshua addresses the issue of oaths, instructing His followers to simply say 'Yes' or 'No'; anything beyond this comes from the evil one.

"You have heard that it was said, 'Do not break your oaths, but fulfil your vows to the Lord.' But I tell you, do not swear at all: not by heaven, because it is God's throne; and not by earth, because it is his footstool; and not by Yerushalayim because it is the city of the great King. And do not swear by your own head since you cannot make one hair white or black. Instead, let your statement be, 'Yes' or 'No' Whatever goes beyond these is from the Evil One".

This teaching underscores the importance of honesty and integrity in all communication. It highlights that the truthfulness demanded by the Ninth Commandment isn't limited to avoiding explicit lies but involves a commitment to genuineness and transparency in all interactions.

Furthermore, Yeshua's denouncement of hypocrisy among the religious leaders of His time illustrates His broader interpretation of bearing false witness. He criticised the Pharisees and teachers of the law for their outward show of piety and adherence to the law while neglecting the more profound demands of justice, mercy, and faithfulness.

"Woe to you, experts in the law and Pharisees, you hypocrites! You give ten percent of your mint, dill, and cumin, but you have neglected the more important matters of the law: justice, mercy, and faith. You should have done these things and not failed to do the other things. Blind guides, you strain out a gnat but swallow a camel!

Woe to you, experts in the law and Pharisees, you hypocrites! You clean the outside of a cup and dish, but inside, they are full of greed and self-indulgence. Blind Pharisees first clean the inside of the cup and dish so that the outside may become clean too.

"Woe to you, experts in the law and Pharisees, you hypocrites! You are like whitewashed tombs that appear beautiful on the outside but on the inside are full of dead people's bones and every kind of uncleanness. In the same way, on the outside, you seem righteous to people, but on the inside, you are full of hypocrisy and wickedness. Matthew 23:23-28

This behaviour is a false witness, as it presents a misleading portrayal of one's relationship with God and others.

Yeshua also emphasised the importance of reconciling with one's brother or sister before offering gifts at the altar.

"So if you are about to offer your gift at the altar, and there you remember that your brother has something against you, leave your gift there in front of the altar and go. First, be reconciled to your brother. Then come and offer your gift". Matthew 5:23-24.

This teaching connects to the Ninth Commandment by highlighting the relationship between truthfulness, reconciliation, and avoiding actions that could falsely represent one's intentions or relationships with others.

The parable of the Good Samaritan further expands on the commandment by illustrating who one's neighbour is and the depth of care and honesty required in our dealings with them.

By portraying a Samaritan, a member of a group despised by the Jews, as the true neighbour because of his compassionate action, Yeshua teaches that bearing faithful witness to one's neighbour involves acts of love, kindness, and mercy that cross societal boundaries.

Yeshua's interactions with individuals also provide insight into how He embodied and taught the principles behind the Ninth Commandment.

For instance, His conversation with the woman at the well (John 4:1-26) demonstrates His commitment to truthfulness. He gently reveals knowledge about her life that leads to a deeper understanding of her spiritual needs and His identity.

While exposing the truth, this interaction does so with grace, offering a model for how truth should be conveyed in a manner that uplifts and transforms rather than condemns.

In all these teachings and actions, Yeshua elevates the Ninth Commandment from a simple legal requirement to a profound ethical principle governing all human interactions. He calls His followers to a life of integrity, where their words and actions are consistently aligned with the truth and their dealings with others reflect the love, respect, and dignity everyone deserves.

Yeshua's reinterpretation of the commandment challenges individuals to examine their actions and the intentions and attitudes that motivate them. Avoiding lying in a narrow sense is not enough; one must cultivate a character marked by honesty, transparency, and a genuine concern for the welfare of others. This approach transforms the commandment from a prohibition against specific wrongful acts into a positive call to live out the values of the Kingdom of God in every aspect of life.

Yeshua's teaching on the Ninth Commandment, "You shall not bear false witness against your neighbour," reveals a comprehensive ethic of truthfulness and integrity. By extending the commandment's application beyond the courtroom to encompass all forms of communication and interaction, He challenges His followers to live lives characterised by honesty, authenticity, and a deep commitment to the well-being of others.

Like all of Yeshua's instructions, this teaching points towards transforming the individual heart as the foundation for a righteous life that honours God and respects the dignity and worth of every person.

How can we follow Yeshua's teaching concerning keeping the ninth commandment, not to bear false witness against your neighbour, in the modern world?

In our modern world of rapid communication and information overload, Yeshua's teachings on the Ninth Commandment,

"You shall not bear false witness against your neighbour" (Exodus 20:16),

resonate more deeply than ever.

While simple in statement, this commandment encompasses a broad spectrum of moral guidance that extends far beyond the courtroom. It's about honesty, integrity, and the respect we owe to others in our speech and actions. In exploring how we can live out this commandment today, we will delve into various scriptural references that illuminate the path of truthfulness Yeshua advocated for.

Yeshua's teachings often went beyond the letter of the law to capture its spirit. In Matthew 5:33-37, He addresses the issue of oaths, emphasising that one should not swear by anything but let their "Yes" be "Yes," and their "No," "No." This teaching underscores the importance of honesty in all our dealings.

Yeshua's point is clear: we should live in such a way that oaths are unnecessary, as our everyday truthfulness should be evidence of our integrity. This perspective challenges us to evaluate how we communicate and to strive for honesty in every word we speak.

Furthermore, in the Parable of the Good Samaritan (Luke 10:25-37), Yeshua expands on the concept of "neighbour" to include anyone in need, regardless of their social or ethnic background.

Just then, an expert in the law stood up to test Yeshua, saying, "Teacher, what must I do to inherit eternal life?"
"What is written in the law?" he asked him. "What do you read there?"
He replied, "Love the Lord your God with all your heart, with all your soul, with all your strength, and with all your mind; and love your neighbour as yourself."
He said to him, "You have answered correctly. Do this, and you will live."
But he wanted to justify himself, so he asked Yeshua, "And who is my neighbour?"
Yeshua replied, "A man was going down from Jerusalem to Jericho. He fell among robbers who stripped him, beat him, and went away, leaving him half dead. It just so happened that a priest was going down that way. But he passed by on the other side when he saw the man. In the same way, a Levite also happened to go there, but when he saw the man, he passed by on the other side. A Samaritan, as he travelled, came to where the man was. When he saw him, he felt sorry for the man. He went to him and bandaged his wounds, pouring oil and wine on them. He put him on his own animal, took him to an inn, and cared for him. The next day, when he left, he took out two denarii, gave them to the innkeeper, and said, 'Take care of him. Whatever extra you spend, I will repay you when I return.' Which of these three do you think acted like a neighbour to the man who fell among robbers?"
"The one who showed mercy to him," he replied.
Then Yeshua told him, "Go and do likewise." Luke 10:25-37

This parable powerfully reminds us that bearing false witness or misleading others can take many forms, not just in legal matters but also in how we talk about and treat those who are different from us.

In today's global village, where cultural misunderstandings can quickly occur, this teaching urges us to seek understanding and to be truthful and kind in our representation of others.

Yeshua's teachings also confront the issue of hypocrisy. In Matthew 23, He rebukes the scribes and Pharisees for their outward show of righteousness, which concealed a lack of true holiness.

This critique is especially relevant in an age when social media often presents a filtered version of reality, encouraging a focus on appearances rather than authenticity. Yeshua's call to integrity challenges us to live authentically and honestly, not just in public but in all aspects of life.

The Epistle of James, reflecting Yeshua's teachings, warns against the dangers of the tongue and the discord it can sow.

Not many of you should become teachers, my brothers, because you know that we who teach will be judged more strictly. To be sure, we all stumble in many ways. If anyone does not stumble in what he says, he is a fully mature man, able to bridle his whole body as well. If we put bits into the mouths of horses so that they will obey us, we also guide the whole animal.

And consider ships: Although they are very big and are driven by fierce winds, they are guided by a very small rudder wherever the pilot wants to go. The tongue is also a small body part, yet it boasts great things.

Consider how a little flame can set a large forest on fire! And the tongue is a fire. It is set among the parts of our body as a world of unrighteousness that stains the whole body, sets the whole course of life on fire, and is set on fire by hell.

Indeed, every kind of animal, bird, reptile, and sea creature is being tamed and has been tamed by mankind. But no one can tame the human tongue. It is a restless evil, full of deadly poison. With it, we bless our Lord and Father, and with it, we curse people who are made in the likeness of God. Blessing and cursing come out of the same mouth.

My brothers, these things should not be this way. Does a spring pour fresh and bitter water from the same opening? Can a fig tree bear olives, or can a grapevine produce figs? A salt spring cannot produce fresh water either.   James 3:1-12

In an era dominated by digital communication, where words can be spread globally in an instant, the wisdom of this caution cannot be overstated. James highlights the power of the tongue to bless and curse, reminding us of the responsibility that comes with our words. This admonition encourages us to use our words to build up rather than tear down, emphasising truth over deceit.

Applying Yeshua's teachings on the Ninth Commandment today means being mindful of how we use our words, whether in person, online, or in any form of communication. It involves checking the accuracy of our information and resisting the temptation to spread rumours or falsehoods, even when it seems harmless or entertaining. It means advocating for truth in a culture that often values convenience or sensationalism over accuracy and depth.

This commandment also involves fostering an environment where honesty is valued and encouraged. This can mean creating spaces in our communities, workplaces, and families where people feel safe speaking the truth without fear of repercussions. It means teaching the next generation the importance of integrity and the courage it takes to stand up for the truth, even when it's not popular.

Moreover, following Yeshua's teachings on this commandment requires us to be compassionate in our truthfulness. Ephesians 4:15 calls us to speak the truth in love, balancing honesty with kindness.

Instead, speaking the truth in love, we will, in every respect, grow up into him, who is the head, the Messiah.

This approach recognises that truth-telling is not just about being right but about building up and nurturing relationships. It's about using our words to heal rather than harm, to bring people together rather than drive them apart.

In a world where fake news and misinformation can spread alarmingly, the call to not bear false witness is more critical than ever. We must be discerning consumers and sharers of information, ensuring that what we pass on is not just true but also beneficial and edifying. This means taking the time to verify facts before spreading them and being willing to correct ourselves and others when misinformation is identified.

Yeshua's emphasis on truth and integrity also challenges us to confront our biases and how they may distort our perception and representation of others. It urges us to look beyond stereotypes and seek the whole story, recognising every person's dignity and worth as a creation of God. This perspective is essential in combating the dehumanisation and division that false narratives can foster.

Following Yeshua's teachings on the Ninth Commandment in today's world is about much more than avoiding outright lies. It's about cultivating a character grounded in truthfulness, integrity, and love.

It's about how we communicate, treat others, and live out our commitment to the truth in every aspect of our lives. We can contribute to a more honest, just, and compassionate world by embracing these teachings.

Chapter 13.

The Tenth Commandment - Understanding the value of what we have.

"You shall not covet your neighbour's house; you shall not covet your neighbour's wife, nor his male servant, nor his female servant, nor his ox, nor his donkey, nor anything that is your neighbour's."

What does Scripture tell us about coveting what our neighbours have?

The tenth commandment is a profound guide that addresses the human inclination to covet what does not belong to us. This commandment,

"You shall not covet your neighbour's house; you shall not covet your neighbour's wife, or his male servant, or his female servant, or his ox, or his donkey, or anything that is your neighbour's"

Exodus 20:17

speaks directly to the heart and mind of an individual. It doesn't merely forbid the physical act of taking what isn't ours but goes deeper, addressing the thoughts and desires that precede any action.

To understand this commandment's gravity and breadth, it's crucial first to grasp what coveting means. Coveting is an intense desire to possess what belongs to someone else. It's more than mere envy or wanting; it's a deep-seated longing that often leads to discontentment with what one has and, at times, results in taking steps to acquire these coveted items unjustly.

The Tenth Commandment is unique among the other commandments in that it explicitly addresses the inner state of a person's heart and mind.

While other commandments, such as not stealing or committing adultery, focus through its words on external actions, this commandment acknowledges that the root of many sins lies in our desires and thoughts. By addressing coveting, Scripture recognises the profound connection between what we harbour in our hearts and the actions that flow from those desires.

Beyond its initial mention in Exodus, the significance of not coveting is further emphasised throughout the Old Testament. For instance, in Deuteronomy 5:21, Moses reiterates the commandment in his sermon to the Israelites, reinforcing its importance in the covenant between God and His people.

This repetition underscores the idea that living a life pleasing to God involves more than just outward compliance with laws; it requires transforming one's inner self.

Coveting can lead to a cascade of other sins. For example, King Ahab's covetousness for Naboth's vineyard (1 Kings 21) led to Naboth's unjust death and brought down God's judgement uponAhab's entire household.

This story illustrates how a covetous heart can lead to profoundly destructive actions for oneself and others. It's a stark reminder that unchecked desire can escalate into actions that violate other commandments, such as stealing or murder.

The wisdom literature in the Old Testament also touches on the issue of covetousness. Proverbs and Ecclesiastes, for example, offer numerous insights into the folly of coveting. They teach that true contentment and happiness are not found in accumulating possessions or envying what others have but in fearing God and finding satisfaction in what He has provided.

"Better is the sight of the eyes than the wandering of the appetite: this also is vanity and a striving after wind." Ecclesiastes 6:9.

This wisdom highlights the emptiness and dissatisfaction that often accompany the pursuit of desires that are not in accordance with God's will.

The prohibition against coveting serves as a moral boundary and a guide for cultivating a heart of gratitude and contentment. By directing our desires toward what is good and aligning our will with God's, we open ourselves to a life marked by peace and satisfaction with what we have. It's about recognising the value of relationships over possessions, appreciating the blessings in our lives, and trusting in God's provision.

Furthermore, the commandment to not covet underscores the importance of community and mutual respect among individuals. We foster a community of trust and mutual respect by respecting the boundaries of what belongs to others, whether property, relationships, or status.

It encourages us to rejoice with others in their blessings rather than resent them to build up the community rather than sow discord and division.

In essence, the Tenth Commandment is a call to introspection and transformation. It challenges us to examine our desires and redirect them in a way that honours God and those around us. This commandment goes beyond the external to touch the very core of our being, inviting us to cultivate a heart that finds its ultimate satisfaction not in the temporal and fleeting but in the eternal and unchanging.

The teaching of the tenth commandment concerning coveting what your neighbour possesses penetrates deep into the human experience. It addresses the root of many sins - our desires - and calls us to a higher standard of living, one centred on contentment, gratitude, and respect for others.

By understanding and applying this commandment, we learn that the key to true fulfilment and peace lies not in acquiring more but in desiring rightly, in harmony with God's will and purposes.

What did Yeshua teach about coveting what our neighbour has?

Yeshua taught profound truths that have echoed through centuries, touching on various aspects of human behaviour and spirituality. Among these teachings, the emphasis on the Tenth Commandment, which advises against coveting our neighbour's possessions, stands out for its deep insight into human desire and the potential for the harm it harbours when misdirected.

Covetousness, at its core, is an intense desire for something that belongs to another. The Tenth Commandment, as presented in the Hebrew Scriptures, specifically Exodus 20:17, admonishes,

"You shall not covet your neighbour's house; you shall not covet your neighbour's wife, or his male servant, or his female servant, or his ox, or his donkey, or anything that is your neighbour's."

This commandment penetrates the heart of human relationships, highlighting the importance of contentment, respect for others' belongings, and the intrinsic value of individuals over material possessions.

Yeshua's teachings often revisited the themes of the Ten Commandments, embedding them within broader spiritual principles. His approach to the Tenth Commandment can be seen as part of his broader message on love, generosity, and the kingdom of God.

Rather than merely restating the commandment, Yeshua delved into the root causes of covetousness, offering a transformative perspective on living in harmony with God's laws.

In the Gospel of Luke 12:15, Yeshua warns,

"Take care, and be on your guard against all covetousness, for one's life does not consist in the abundance of his possessions."

Yeshua points out the futility of measuring life's worth by material accumulation, a direct commentary on the dangers of coveting. This statement reinforces the Tenth Commandment and redirects focus towards spiritual wealth and the value of relationships over possessions.

Yeshua's parable of the Rich Fool, (Luke 12:16-21), serves as a powerful illustration of his teaching against covetousness. The story recounts a rich man who, after a bountiful harvest, decides to tear down his barns to build larger ones to store all his grain and goods. He tells himself that he can rest, eat, drink, and be merry.

However, God calls him a fool because his life is demanded of him that night, and he has stored up treasure for himself but is not rich toward God.

This narrative warns against the greed that leads to coveting and emphasises the importance of seeking spiritual riches over accumulating material wealth.

Moreover, in Matthew 6:19-21, Yeshua advises,

"Do not lay up for yourselves treasures on earth, where moth andrust destroy and where thieves break in and steal, but lay up for yourselves treasures in heaven, where neither moth nor rust

destroys and where thieves do not break in and steal. For where your treasure is, there your heart will be also."

This teaching directly confronts the desire to covet earthly possessions by encouraging a focus on eternal, spiritual values. It implies that covetousness misaligns our priorities, drawing our hearts away from God and towards transient, material things.

Yeshua's emphasis on the internal rather than the external is further highlighted in his teachings on purity of heart and intention. In Matthew 5:8, He declares,

"Blessed are the pure in heart, for they shall see God."

While this beatitude does not directly mention covetousness, it speaks to the condition of the heart that covets what others have. A pure heart is free from the desire to possess what belongs to others, and such purity brings one closer to God.

Another significant aspect of Yeshua's teaching is the Great Commandment, which encapsulates the essence of the law and the prophets: to love God with all your heart, soul, and mind, and to love your neighbour as yourself (Matthew 22:37-40).

Loving one's neighbour as oneself is fundamentally incompatible with covetousness. If we truly love our neighbours, we would not covet their possessions, as such desires can lead to harm and discord.

Yeshua's confrontation with the rich young ruler (Mark 10:17-22) also sheds light on the issue of covetousness. The young man claims to have kept all the commandments from his youth, yet when Yeshua tells him to sell all he has, give to the poor, and follow Him, the young man goes away sorrowful, for he had great possessions. This encounter illustrates how the desire for wealth and possessions can hinder one's relationship with God and others.

Yeshua's teachings on the Tenth Commandment challenge us to examine our hearts and our relationship with material possessions. He calls for radically reevaluating values and encourages a life focused on love, generosity, and spiritual richness. Covetousness, rooted in desire and comparison, is revealed as a barrier to true fulfilment and harmony with God's will.

Through His words and parables, Yeshua invites us to live in a way that transcends mere adherence to commandments, aiming for a transformation of the heart. He offers freedom from the chains of covetousness, opening the door to a life of joy, peace, and true contentment. His teachings remind us that our worth is not measured by our possessions but by the love we share and the lives we touch.

How are we to follow Yeshua's teaching about not being covetous in the modern world?

In today's fast-paced world, where the pursuit of success, material wealth, and personal happiness often takes precedence, the teachings of Yeshua on covetousness towards our neighbour offer a timeless guide to living a more fulfilled and ethical life.

Covetousness, the intense desire to possess what belongs to another, can lead to adverse outcomes, from personal dissatisfaction and strained relationships to broader societal issues. By exploring Yeshua's teachings on this topic, we can uncover practical advice for modern living that promotes generosity, contentment, and empathy.

First and foremost, it's important to understand that at the heart of avoiding covetousness is the practice of contentment. In a world bombarded with advertisements and social media highlights showcasing the latest gadgets, luxury vacations, and picture-perfect lifestyles, it's easy to fall into the trap of believing that happiness and fulfilment come from acquiring more.

Modern advertising often employs sophisticated psychological strategies designed to cultivate a deep-seated desire for products or lifestyles that may be beyond one's means or necessities.

By showcasing idealised lifestyles, unattainable beauty standards, or the latest, must-have products, advertisements can instil a sense of inadequacy or longing in consumers.

This constant exposure to what one should have, but does not, fosters an attitude of covetousness, where the desire to possess what others have overshadows contentment with what one already possesses.

Through the manipulation of emotions and the exploitation of social comparison, modern advertising not only drives consumer behaviour but also subtly encourages a culture of never-ending desire and competition for more, often at the expense of personal satisfaction and happiness.

However, Yeshua's teachings guide us to find joy and satisfaction in what we already have. This doesn't mean we shouldn't strive for improvement or feel pleased with new acquisitions, but rather that we should not let our happiness depend solely on external possessions.

Practising gratitude is a powerful tool in this regard. By regularly reflecting on and being thankful for the blessings in our lives, such as health, relationships, and even simple pleasures, we can foster a sense of contentment that diminishes the desire to covet what others have.

Moreover, Yeshua's teachings encourage us to focus on the well-being of others rather than merely our own desires. In today's individualistic society, it's easy to prioritise personal gain over the needs and feelings of our neighbours.

However, embracing a mindset of generosity and service can lead to deeper, more meaningful connections and a more harmonious community. This can be as simple as offering our time to listen to a friend in need, donating to those less fortunate, or volunteering for community service. When we shift our focus from what we want to what we can give, we adhere to Yeshua's teachings and find greater purpose and fulfilment in our lives.

Furthermore, Yeshua's stance on covetousness invites us to cultivate empathy and understanding toward others. In a world where judgement and comparison are commonplace, it is revolutionary to practise seeing the world from our neighbour's perspective.

Recognising that everyone has their own struggles, dreams, and paths can help us appreciate their successes and empathise with their challenges instead of feeling envious or resentful. This approach reduces covetous feelings and builds stronger, more compassionate relationships.

Additionally, Yeshua's teachings on covetousness challenge us to reconsider our definition of success. In a society that often equates success with financial wealth, social status, or professional achievements, it's easy to covet these markers when observed in others.

However, by redefining success to include personal growth, the quality of our relationships, and our impact on the world around us, we can pursue goals that are more aligned with our deepest values. This perspective shift can alleviate the pressure to constantly compare ourselves to others and instead focus on living a life that is true to ourselves and our beliefs.

Practically speaking, avoiding covetousness also means being mindful of the media we consume and the influences we allow into our lives. Social media, in particular, can be a breeding ground for feelings of inadequacy and desire for what others have.

By consciously curating our media consumption to include uplifting, inspirational, or educational content, we can guard our hearts and minds against the seeds of covetousness. This might involve unfollowing accounts that trigger feelings of envy, seeking out stories of kindness and generosity, or limiting screen time to make room for real-life connections and experiences.

Yeshua's teachings on covetousness also encourage us to embrace simplicity and sustainability. Pursuing more can have dire consequences for our planet in a world facing environmental challenges and resource scarcity.

By choosing to live more simply, making mindful decisions about our consumption, and prioritising the well-being of the environment, we follow Yeshua's teachings and contribute to a healthier, more sustainable world. This could mean opting for experiences over possessions, recycling and reusing when possible, and supporting ethical and environmentally friendly businesses and products.

Lastly, embracing Yeshua's teachings on covetousness calls for a commitment to personal reflection and growth. Regularly examining our thoughts, motivations, and actions can help us identify when covetousness is creeping into our lives and guide us back to a path of gratitude, generosity, and contentment. Reflecting on our spiritual and ethical journey, whether through prayer, meditation, journaling, or conversation with trusted friends or mentors, is crucial for living out these teachings in our daily lives.

Yeshua's teachings on covetousness in today's world involve a multifaceted approach that touches every aspect of life, from our personal mindset and relationships to our impact on society and the planet.

By cultivating contentment, focusing on giving rather than receiving, practising empathy, redefining success, being mindful of our influences, embracing simplicity, and committing to personal growth, we can navigate the challenges of modern life with integrity and purpose.

While it's not always easy to resist the pull of covetousness in a world that often encourages it, the rewards of living in alignment with these teachings are profound and far-reaching, leading to a life of genuine happiness, deeper connections, and a positive impact on the world around us.

Chapter 14.

A Recap of the Main Points.

"The Wisdom of Yeshua: How Our Inner World Shapes Our Outer Actions"

Yeshua's teachings, especially those focused on the Ten Commandments, offer a profound exploration into societal and individual morality and spirituality. Rather than advocating for a strict, literal adherence to these ancient decrees, His perspective encourages a deeper, more introspective approach.

In his teachings on each commandment, Yeshua emphasises the condition of the heart and mind. He suggests that the essence of these commandments is not in their literal observance but in the individual's underlying intentions and attitudes.

By examining His interpretations, we uncover that Yeshua often expanded upon the original commandments to include thoughts and feelings as integral components of sin or righteousness. For instance, He taught that anger towards another could be equated with the act of murder in one's heart, or that looking at someone with lustful intent was akin to committing adultery in the heart.

Through this lens, it becomes apparent that He aimed to shift focus from external actions to internal motivations, highlighting that faithful obedience to God's laws begins within the inner moral and spiritual state.

This nuanced understanding of the commandments underlines a broader message about the sources of societal and individual issues. Yeshua suggests that problems such as injustice, violence, and immorality stem not from the lack of external compliance with the law but from the flawed internal landscape of the human heart and mind. He posits that a transformation within these internal realms is essential for true spiritual fulfilment and societal harmony.

Yeshua's teachings have profound implications for individuals and society. On a personal level, individuals are called to cultivate an inner life of purity, integrity, and compassion, recognising that true righteousness is a matter of the heart and mind.

Societally, these teachings encourage communities to look beyond mere legal compliance and foster environments where virtues such as empathy, understanding, and peace are prioritised.

In essence, Yeshua's expansion on the Ten Commandments invites a re-evaluation of our moral compasses, encouraging a shift towards internal spiritual alignment as the foundation for ethical living and societal well-being.

The First Commandment: No Other Gods.

The First Commandment firmly establishes the principle of monotheism - the worship of one God. This foundational commandment sets the tone for the relationship between the divine and humanity, making it clear that the worship, love, and allegiance of the faithful should be directed exclusively towards the one true God.

Yeshua, in His teachings, particularly in Matthew 22:37, amplifies and deepens the understanding of this commandment by instructing His followers to

"love God with all your heart, with all your soul, and with all your mind."

This command to love God comprehensively encompasses every

aspect of human existence - emotional, spiritual, and intellectual. It suggests that obedience to God and the commitment to Him should not be superficial or limited to external rituals, but should penetrate to the very core of our being.

In emphasising love for God as the greatest commandment, Yeshua highlights the relational aspect of the commandment. It's notmerely about the avoidance of worshipping other gods in a physical sense, such as idols made of wood or stone, but it extends to the internal world of desires, priorities, and thoughts.

Anything that takes precedence over God in our hearts - be it wealth, power, relationships, or even our own egos - can become a form of idolatry. This interpretation underscores the belief that idolatry isn't just an ancient or physical act; it's a matter of the heart and mind, relevant to every generation.

The consequences of idolatry, as implied in the teachings of Yeshua, go beyond individual sin. When our ultimate love and devotion are misdirected, it doesn't only affect our relationship with God; it also leads to societal and personal degradation.

Idolatry can manifest in various forms of moral and ethical corruption, such as injustice, greed, and the exploitation of the vulnerable. By misplacing our devotion, we create societies that reflect these disordered loves, rather than the kingdom of God, which is founded on righteousness, justice, and love.

Therefore, the call to love God with all one's heart, soul, and mind is not only about personal piety but also about shaping a community that mirrors divine virtues. It's a call to examine what we value most, to reorder our lives in a way that places God at the centre, and to participate in the building of a world that reflects His goodness, truth, and beauty.

This deeper understanding of the First Commandment invites us into a transformative relationship with God, where our desires, thoughts, and affections are aligned with His will, leading to a life of true fulfilment and purpose.

The Second Commandment: No Idols

In discussing the interpretation of the Second Commandment through the lens of Yeshua's teachings, it's essential to delve deeper into the nuanced understanding of idolatry.

Traditionally, the Second Commandment forbids the creation and worship of physical idols, a straightforward directive aimed at preventing the veneration of any entity or object besides the divine.

However, Yeshua's insights offer a profound expansion of this commandment, emphasising the internal aspects of idolatry rather than merely its external manifestations.

Yeshua teaches that idolatry extends beyond the tangible act of creating or worshipping an image; it encompasses the allocation of one's heart, mind, and resources to something other than the divine.

This perspective reveals that whatever dominates our thoughts, affections, and endeavours essentially assumes the role of an idol in our lives. It might not be a graven image, but its effect on our spiritual and moral compass is no less significant. This could be anything from an obsessive pursuit of wealth, status, power, or even relationships that detract from one's spiritual commitments.

The core of Yeshua's teaching is the realisation that idolatry is fundamentally an issue of misplaced devotion. It's about where one's loyalties, desires, and priorities truly lie. When anything other than the divine commands our primary focus, it not only becomes an idol but also leads us away from a spiritually centred life.

This misplaced devotion has far-reaching implications, manifesting in societal issues such as materialism, consumerism, and the relentless pursuit of power. These are not merely economic or social concerns but are symptomatic of a deeper spiritual malaise.

Materialism and consumerism, for example, reflect a society's collective prioritisation of wealth and possessions over spiritual or relational values. The incessant drive for more, fueled by a culture that equates success with material accumulation, mirrors the individual's internal state of idolatry.

Similarly, the pursuit of power and status often reveals a deep-seated need for recognition and control, overshadowing the humility and service that are central to spiritual growth.

Yeshua's interpretation of the Second Commandment challenges individuals to examine their lives critically, identifying what truly occupies the central place in their hearts. It's a call to introspection and transformation, urging a realignment of our priorities, affections, and endeavours towards the divine.

This shift not only addresses the root of personal spiritual struggles but also has the potential to transform societal values, steering them away from shallow materialism and towards deeper, more meaningful pursuits.

The Third Commandment: Misusing God's Name

Yeshua's teachings regarding not taking the Lord's name in vain offer a profound understanding that goes far beyond the simple prohibition of misusing God's name in speech. This commandment, deeply rooted in respect and reverence for the divine, emphasises the importance of aligning one's life with the values and character of God. It calls for integrity, a virtue that demands consistency between what one professes to believe and how one acts in the world.

The principle of not taking the Lord's name in vain is not just about avoiding certain words or phrases; it's about embodying the essence of what it means to be a follower of God.

This includes acts of kindness, justice, mercy, and humility - qualities that reflect God's nature. When individuals claim to have faith, yet their actions betray selfishness, injustice, or cruelty, they not only dishonour the name of God but also undermine the very foundation of their professed beliefs.

The discrepancy between professing faith and living it out has significant consequences, both personally and collectively. On a personal level, it leads to a fractured identity, where the external and internal selves are in conflict. For societies, this hypocrisy can result in moral decay, where the outward appearance of religiosity masks underlying injustices and inequalities. It creates an environment where words lose their meaning and faith becomes superficial, eroding trust and community cohesion.

Yeshua's call to live in a way that does not take the Lord's name in vain, therefore, is a call to authenticity and transformation. It challenges individuals and communities to reflect on their actions and to strive for a life that truly embodies the principles of their faith. By doing so, they honour God not just with their words, but with their entire being, contributing to the creation of a more just and compassionate world.

The Fourth Commandment: The Sabbath

In his teachings, Yeshua offers a transformative interpretation of the Sabbath commandment that extends far beyond the conventional understanding of rest. He challenged the prevailing legalistic approaches of his time, which often reduced the observance of the Sabbath to a rigid set of rules, potentially losing sight of its deeper significance.

The Gospel of Mark, particularly in 2:27, captures the essence of Yeshua's perspective:

"The Sabbath was made for man, not man for the Sabbath."

This statement underscores the idea that the Sabbath is not an end in itself but a means to foster human well-being and spiritual growth.

Yeshua's view of the Sabbath as a liberating force emerges from his broader mission to free humanity from all forms of bondage - be it sin, sickness, social injustice, or religious legalism.

By healing the sick and extending mercy on the Sabbath, he demonstrates that the day is meant to bring life and wholeness to individuals and communities. These acts of compassion emphasise the Sabbath's role in breaking down the barriers that separate people from the fullness of life and from one another.

Furthermore, Yeshua highlights the Sabbath as a time for reflection and reconnection with God. This sacred pause in the week serves as a reminder of human limitations and the need to rely on the Divine.

It's a time to step away from the incessant demands of work and society, to contemplate the goodness of creation, and to nurture a relationship with God. This practice cultivates humility, acknowledging that human efforts are not sufficient without divine sustenance, and gratitude, recognizing the abundance of God's provision.

By framing the Sabbath in this way, Yeshua advocates for a society that values compassion over compliance, and relationship overregulation. This ethos encourages a community grounded in humility, recognizing that all are dependent on God's grace, and gratitude, celebrating the gift of rest and renewal. Such a community is better equipped to act justly and love mercy, embodying the liberating spirit of the Sabbath in all aspects of life.

The Fifth Commandment: Honour Your Parents

In this passage, Yeshua delves into the critical and nuanced teachings around honouring one's parents, as commanded in the Ten Commandments.

Yet, He goes further by addressing a concerning practice of His time, where individuals would declare their possessions as 'Corban' (a gift devoted to God), thereby legally exempting themselves from using these resources to support their parents.

For Moses said, 'Honour your father and your mother,' and, 'He who speaks evil of father or mother must be put to death.' But you say if anyone tells his father or mother, 'Whatever you might have gained from me is an offering to God, then you no longer permit him to do anything for his father or mother, making void the word of God with your tradition that you've handed down."
Mark 7:10-13

This act, while outwardly appearing pious, covertly circumvented the moral and ethical obligation to care for one's ageing parents.

Yeshua condemns this behaviour, highlighting the hypocrisy of adhering to religious traditions and rituals while neglecting the underlying principles of love, respect, and familial responsibility.

The critique Yeshua offers transcends the immediate context, pointing to a broader societal issue. The act of honouring one's parents is not merely a legalistic requirement but an expression of respect, empathy, and genuine care.

These values should emanate from a heart and mind deeply rooted in love and a sense of duty towards one's family and community. Yeshua emphasises that genuine faith is demonstrated through actions that reflect God's love and care for individuals, especially those in need of support, such as the elderly.

Furthermore, the passage serves as a poignant commentary on the broader societal implications of neglecting such fundamental values. Societal neglect of the elderly and the disintegration of family structures are symptomatic of a collective heart that has grown cold to the needs of others.

This condition speaks to a deeper spiritual malaise, where the emphasis on external religious observances overshadows the core biblical teachings of love, compassion, and responsibility towards one another.

In essence, Yeshua's teachings call for a reevaluation of priorities, urging individuals and societies to cultivate a heart attuned to love and responsibility. By doing so, we can address the deeper issues of familial neglect and societal disregard for the elderly, fostering a community use that upholds the dignity and worth of every member, particularly those who are most vulnerable.

The Sixth Commandment: Do Not Murder

In the Sermon on the Mount, Yeshua presents a revolutionary reinterpretation of traditional Jewish law, taking the commandment "Thou shalt not kill" to a deeper, more introspective level.

In Matthew 5:21-22, He challenges His listeners by equating the internal state of anger with the act of murder, suggesting that the sin begins in the heart long before it is manifested in actions.

This teaching emphasises the importance of monitoring and controlling one's inner emotional state, recognizing that unchecked anger and resentment can lead to serious conflict and violence.

Yeshua's message goes beyond mere behaviour modification; He seeks a transformation of the heart. He identifies anger and resentment as not just personal failings but as the root causes of societal violence and conflict.

By harbouring such negative emotions, individuals contribute to a culture of aggression and misunderstanding. Therefore, the pathway to peace - both internal and within society - lies in cultivating a heart of forgiveness and understanding.

This approach calls for individuals to address and resolve their internal turmoil through self-reflection and active forgiveness, thereby preventing such emotions from escalating into physical harm or violent actions.

Furthermore, Yeshua's teachings suggest that this internal transformation is not just about avoiding negative outcomes but about building a foundation for positive, compassionate interactions with others.

By promoting a culture of understanding and forgiveness,

communities can mitigate the cycle of violence and aggression, leading to more harmonious relationships and a more peaceful society.

This perspective encourages individuals to look inward for the sources of external conflict and to make personal changes that have far-reaching effects on their interactions with others and the world at large.

The Seventh Commandment: No Adultery

In the Sermon on the Mount, as recounted in Matthew 5:27-28, Yeshua presents a profound expansion on the traditional understanding of the commandment against adultery. He states,

"You have heard that it was said, 'You shall not commit adultery.' But I tell you that anyone who looks at a woman lustfully has already committed adultery with her in his heart."

This statement shifts the focus from mere actions to the intentions and desires that precede them, emphasising that the moral and ethical foundation of a person's actions begins deep within their thoughts and feelings.

This deeper interpretation underscores the importance of self-discipline, not only in actions but also in the inner workings of the mind and heart.

It suggests that the battle against sin, such as adultery, is not merely a matter of avoiding the physical act but also involves mastering one's desires and redirecting them towards what is righteous and good.

This aligns with a broader principle seen throughout Yeshua's teachings: the transformation of the inner person to produce outward behaviours that reflect justice, love, and truth.

In applying this teaching to the context of fidelity in relationships, it becomes clear that true faithfulness extends beyond physical loyalty to include the purity of one's thoughts and desires towards others. It calls for a comprehensive integrity that encompasses both deed and intention, pointing towards a holistic understanding of faithfulness that nurtures trust and respect within relationships.

Moreover, Yeshua's teaching has implications for a broader societal commitment to justice and truth. It suggests that societal issues, such as injustice and falsehood, can also be traced back to the desires and intentions harboured by individuals.

As such, cultivating a culture of integrity and truthfulness requires more than just external regulations and punishments; it necessitates a collective effort to discipline and purify the desires of the heart, aligning them with principles of righteousness and love.

In this way, Yeshua's expansion on the prohibition of adultery serves as a call to personal and societal transformation. It invites individuals to examine and discipline their inner life, aligning their desires with values that promote fidelity, justice, and truth.

Through this inner transformation, the hope is that individuals will not only avoid sin but also contribute to the creation of a more just and loving society.

The Eighth Commandment: Do Not Steal

In expanding upon Yeshua's teaching, it's important to delve deeper into the understanding that the commandment against stealing encompasses more than just the physical act of theft.

Yeshua emphasises that before the act of stealing occurs, there is often a profound sense of covetousness - a deep longing or desire for what belongs to another. This covetousness is not merely a precursor to the act of theft; it is an ailment of the soul that distorts human desires and priorities.

The issue at hand is not solely the external behaviours of theft and corruption observable in society. Rather, these behaviours are symptomatic of a much deeper issue - a malady characterised by discontent and greed.

In a society where individuals are constantly seeking more, dissatisfied with what they have, and envious of others' possessions or achievements, theft and corruption become more prevalent. This cycle of discontent and greed not only damages the social fabric but also distances individuals from a sense of community and shared humanity.

To address this fundamental problem, Yeshua suggests that the remedy lies in cultivating contentment and generosity within the human heart.

Contentment is the state of being satisfied with what one has, recognizing and appreciating the value of one's own life and possessions without constantly seeking more. It involves an inner peace and acceptance that diminishes the impulse to covet what belongs to others.

Generosity, on the other hand, is the willingness to give freely, not just in terms of material possessions but also in love, time, and support. It is an outward expression of an inner attitude of abundance and empathy.

By fostering generosity, individuals can transcend self-centred desires, contributing to the wellbeing of others and, in turn, strengthening the bonds of community.

Yeshua's teachings suggest that the path to healing a society afflicted by theft and corruption lies not in stricter enforcement of laws or more severe punishments, but in a transformation of the human heart.

By nurturing contentment and generosity, individuals can create a culture that values mutual respect, compassion, and the common good over personal gain.

This shift in values is essential for building a society where theft and corruption are not merely suppressed, but are made irrelevant by the abundance of shared contentment and generosity.

The Ninth Commandment: No False Testimony

Yeshua's teachings emphasise the importance of honesty, not just in our words but as a fundamental aspect of our being. He states that dishonesty - bearing false witness - is not merely an external act, but one that originates from a deeper place within us: the heart and mind.

This insight highlights how personal integrity is crucial, suggesting that deceitful actions and words are symptoms of inner discord and a lack of alignment with the truth.

The relevance of Yeshua's call becomes even more apparent when considering the broader societal implications. Misinformation, slander, and deceit are not merely individual failings but reflect a collective movement away from a culture of truthfulness. These issues, prevalent in many aspects of modern society, from media to personal interactions, undermine trust and cohesion, leading to division and conflict.

Addressing these societal challenges requires more than just surface-level solutions. It necessitates a foundational shift back towards sincerity and integrity, virtues Yeshua deeply advocated for.

This return is not just about avoiding falsehood but embracing a way of life that values and upholds truth in all forms. It involves each individual examining their own beliefs and behaviours, striving for consistency between their inner values and outward actions, and fostering communities where honesty is cherished and practised.

This holistic approach not only benefits the individual, fostering peace and authenticity, but also has the potential to transform society, creating a more trustworthy and harmonious world.

The Tenth Commandment: Do Not Covet

Finally, Yeshua's teachings on covetousness delve deep into the root causes of societal discontent and interpersonal strife. By advocating for contentment and a steadfast trust in God's provision, as highlighted in Luke 12:15, He directly confronts the pervasive and insidious nature of greed. This verse,

"Take care, and be on your guard against all covetousness, for one's life does not consist in the abundance of his possessions,"

encapsulates His message that true fulfilment and happiness cannot be found in the relentless accumulation of material wealth. This principle challenges the very fabric of societal norms and values that often glorify wealth and success as the ultimate indicators of a person's worth.

Yeshua's stance on this issue is not merely a moral or ethical directive but a profound spiritual teaching that seeks to realign human desires towards more meaningful and eternal pursuits.

By cautioning against covetousness, He is not only addressing the direct impact such desires have on one's character and spiritual health but also how they contribute to wider social inequalities. The incessant desire for more can lead to exploitation, injustice,and neglect of the vulnerable, as individuals and systems prioritise wealth accumulation over equitable distribution and the well-being of all community members.

Furthermore, by promoting trust in God's provision, Yeshua introduces an alternative paradigm of dependency and security. This trust is not a passive resignation but an active engagement with faith, where individuals are encouraged to seek their value and sustenance beyond the material, placing their lives and hopes in the hands of a provident God.

This shift in perspective not only fosters individual peace and satisfaction but also encourages a communal ethic of generosity and care, directly challenging the divisions and disparities fostered by covetous attitudes.

Thus, Yeshua's teachings on covetousness and contentment offer a transformative vision for society - one rooted in values of trust, generosity, and a profound sense of community over individual gain.

By addressing the root of personal dissatisfaction and societal strife, He invites individuals and communities to envision and work towards a world where true contentment and equality are pursued over transient and divisive desires.

Conclusion

Yeshua's reinterpretation of the Ten Commandments goes beyond a simple call to adhere to a set of external regulations; it represents a profound shift towards understanding the essence and spirit of these laws as integral to the fabric of our inner lives.

He identifies the root of many societal and personal challenges as not just the actions we undertake but the thoughts and intentions that precede them.

By emphasising the importance of what happens within the human heart and mind, Yeshua underscores the belief that true adherence to these commandments requires more than just outward conformity; it necessitates a deep, internal transformation of one's character and desires.

This internal focus does not diminish the importance of the commandments as guidelines for moral behaviour but elevates them to a tool for spiritual and personal growth.

Yeshua teaches that the commandments are not merely a checklist for righteousness but a roadmap for cultivating a heart and mind aligned with divine principles. This alignment involves a radical shift from self-centeredness to a love that encompasses God and extends to others, reflecting a holistic approach to spirituality that transcends mere rule-following.

In proposing this inward journey, Yeshua invites individuals to engage in a process of self-examination, repentance, and renewal. This process is not isolated to individual transformation but is seen as essential for societal healing and progress.

By fostering a community of individuals who live out these principles from the inside out, Yeshua envisions a society transformed by love, justice, and peace.

Therefore, the teachings of the Ten Commandments, as reinterpreted by Yeshua, offer not just a path to personal spiritual renewal but a blueprint for building a more compassionate and equitable world.

In essence, Yeshua's message emphasises that the journey toward a righteous life and a harmonious society begins not with external adherence to laws but with an internal transformation of the heart and mind.

This perspective shifts the focus from religious obligation to spiritual awakening, offering a path to true peace and fulfilment that begins within each individual and radiates outward, influencing every aspect of human interaction and societal structure.

Chapter 15.

A Compassionate Shift: The Impact of Living by the Ten Commandments Today, Yeshua's Way.

Having read this far and considered the teachings of Yeshua on the Ten Commandments, try taking a moment, maybe in the quiet of the morning or during a reflective evening, and consider,

"What if society wholeheartedly embraced the Ten Commandments, in the way Yeshua interpreted and taught them? Not just driven to be obedient by the actions we undertake, but by the thoughts, intentions and motivation that precede them?"

Imagine with me for a moment, and let's not confine this to merely a religious musing. Rather, let's approach it as a profound exploration into how these ancient guidelines, if genuinely followed, could revolutionise our contemporary world.

Think of it as peering through a lens at the potential monumental impact these enduring tenets could unleash on our day-to-day lives and societal structures.Now, I'm not suggesting we view this through rose-coloured glasses, pretending that implementing such a change would be simple or without its challenges. However, the thought itself is fascinating, isn't it?

Let's dive into this idea, considering not only the obvious shifts but the subtle ripples such adherence would create across the fabric of our society. What kind of transformations could we witness in our interactions, our laws, our overall moral compass, and our physical and mental well-being if these principles were at the heart of all our actions?

Picture a world where respect and love for one another aren't idealistic goals but lived realities. Where honesty, integrity, and kindness aren't rarities but the norm.

Envision communities where the emphasis is on cooperation and understanding rather than competition and division. Think about the implications for issues like crime, corruption, and even personal relationships.

So, grab your favourite cosy beverage, settle in, and let's embark on this thought-provoking exploration together. We'll muse over the possible changes in societal attitudes towards possession, respect for life and property, and the overall sense of community and connection.

This isn't just about dreaming of a utopia but engaging in a serious conversation about the profound impact embracing such foundational principles could have on our world. Let's consider the potential, the pitfalls, and everything in between.

In the grand tapestry of human history, the commandment *"Love thy neighbour"* has echoed through the ages, but Yeshua cranked up the volume, transforming it from a whispered moral directive into a thunderous call to action.

Imagine a society radically reshaped by this principle. This wouldn't be a world where *"Love thy neighbour"* is just a bumper sticker but a living, breathing ethos infiltrating every aspect of communal life.

In such a society, the concept of community takes on a whole new dimension. It's a place where everyone, regardless of race, religion, or the size of their bank account, actively looks out for one another.

Here, acts of kindness and generosity aren't sporadic events that make the evening news; they're as routine as the sunrise. People don't just coexist; they genuinely care for and support each other, creating a robust safety net that leaves no one dangling on the margins.

Imagine neighbourhoods where the idea of leaving someone behind because of their background or financial status is frowned upon and unthinkable. In this utopia, the stark divisions that currently slice through our society, segregating us into isolated silos, would start to crumble.

The barriers erected by prejudice, misunderstanding, and fear would gradually be dismantled, brick by brick, replaced by bridges of mutual respect and understanding.

This is not just a pipe dream but a possible reality. Acts of kindness, large and small, would weave a vibrant landscape of human connection.

Instead of being polarised by our differences, we'd celebrate them, recognising that diversity is not a threat but a treasure trove of perspectives, ideas, and experiences enriching us all. Our world would be a kaleidoscope of cultures and beliefs, where understanding and empathy illuminate the shadows of ignorance and intolerance.

In this revolutionised society, *"Love thy neighbour"* becomes the golden thread that binds us, guiding our actions and interactions. It's a principle that encourages us to look beyond ourselves, to see the humanity in others, and to act with compassion and empathy.

By embracing this ethos, we'd transform our immediate communities and send ripples of change cascading through the wider world, heralding a new era of human relations grounded in genuine love and respect for all.

In today's fast-paced world, where the truth often blurs between the lines of fact and fiction, the age-old commandment against bearing false witness holds a power that could radically transform the very fabric of our society.

Imagine, if you will, a world where honesty isn't just encouraged but is the unbreakable rule, the gold standard by which we all operate. This isn't just about avoiding lies; it's about embracing truth as the foundation of all our personal, professional, or political interactions.

Let's picture how this seismic shift in attitude and behaviour could revolutionise our personal lives. Friendships and romantic relationships, often mired in misunderstandings and unnecessary heartaches due to deceit, would flourish under the warm sunlight of transparency. The fear of betrayal would fade, replaced by a deep sense of security, knowing that honesty is not just expected but guaranteed.

Transitioning to the business world, consider the profound impact on consumer confidence and corporate reputation if honesty were the unwavering standard. Companies wouldn't compete on the quality of their products or the efficiency of their services but on their integrity and truthfulness.

Trust becomes the cornerstone of every transaction and interaction in such an environment. The marketplace would be transformed into a vibrant ecosystem where genuine trust isn't just a rare commodity but the norm, fostering an era of unparalleled innovation and growth.

But why stop there? Extend this vision to politics, where honesty is often perceived as a liability rather than an asset. If politicians were held to this standard of unwavering truthfulness, political discourse would be elevated from the murky depths of manipulation and misinformation to a platform for genuine debate and meaningful progress.

Campaigns would no longer hinge on who can spin the most convincing narrative but on who has the best ideas and the most sincere commitment to public service. In this world, voter cynicism would give way to renewed engagement and optimism about the potential for real change.

Making honesty a non-negotiable aspect of our lives would render lying as obsolete as dial-up internet. No longer would we have to navigate a world where deceit lurks around every corner, sowing distrust and confusion. Instead, we'd live in a society where honesty is not just the best policy but the only policy, creating a legacy of trust for future generations to inherit and build upon.

So, as we ponder the possibilities, it becomes clear that the power of truth extends far beyond the moral high ground. It has the potential to heal divisions, build bridges, and propel us forward into a future where honesty is the currency of trust, universally valued and meticulously upheld.

In this world, we're not just avoiding falsehood; we're actively cultivating a culture of integrity, transparency, and respect - a world where honesty is the best policy in every sense.

Amid our fast-paced, constantly connected world, where the lines between work and rest blur, the age-old directive to *"Remember the Sabbath day, to keep it holy"* emerges not just as a religious observance but as a profound reminder of the need for a pause.

With its relentless demand for productivity and connectivity, our society often forgets the importance of stepping back, taking a deep breath, and truly disconnecting from the myriad of screens that dominate our lives.

This commandment invites us to consider a radical shift in how we view our time. It's not merely about taking a day off from the hustle and bustle of work but about intentionally setting aside time to focus on what genuinely enriches our lives.

Imagine a day when the only notifications we receive are from family members asking how we are or friends inviting us for a leisurely walk in the park. A day where, instead of scrolling through endless feeds of information, we engage in conversations that nourish the soul and activities that rejuvenate the body.

Adopting such a practice is more than personal relaxation; it would cultivate a culture that values and prioritises well-being and mental health. In doing so, we acknowledge that our worth is not measured by our productivity but by the quality of our relationships and the depth of our connection to ourselves and the world around us.

By reclaiming this time, we also reconnect with the fundamentals of human existence that modern life often overlooks. Whether it's savouring a meal with loved ones without the urge to check emails, enjoying the simple beauty of nature, or indulging in hobbies that bring joy, these moments of rest and reflection are essential to our well-being.

The call to "keep the Sabbath holy" is a call to reclaim our time for what truly matters. It encourages us to pause, reflect, and make conscious choices about spending our hours and days. In a world that often feels like it's moving too fast, a dedicated day of rest can be a sanctuary of peace and a reminder of the joys and connections that make life worth living.

In the contemporary world, characterised by its quick pace, where instant gratification often takes precedence, it's easy to overlook the timeless wisdom of ancient commandments, particularly those addressing adultery and coveting. These principles serve as foundational blocks, urging us to honour and respect the boundaries of others, not just in our romantic relationships but also in how we view and treat their possessions.

Yeshua's teachings bring a deeper dimension to these commandments, emphasising the importance of the heart's intentions behind our actions. He invites us to look inward, evaluate our motivations, and cultivate a genuine respect for the sanctity of personal relationships and a sense of contentment with what we already possess.

This perspective is not just about adhering to a set of rules; it's about fostering an internal moral compass that guides us toward integrity and away from harm.

Imagine the transformative impact this shift in mindset could have on our society. Relationships, the very fabric of our communities, would be strengthened as individuals learn to value and honour their commitments to one another. Families would become more stable and cohesive, fortified by trust and mutual respect. This, in turn, would contribute to building healthier, more resilient communities where individuals feel supported and connected.

Moreover, this renewed emphasis on respect and contentment could play a pivotal role in reducing crime rates. Many criminal acts stem from a desire to obtain what belongs to others, whether it's their property, their sense of security, their peace of mind or even their identity. By cultivating a society that values contentment with one's own and respect for others' boundaries, we address these issues at their root, fostering a safer, more peaceful environment for all.

In such a society, the emphasis on material possessions would wane, giving way to a culture that values people over things. This shift in priorities could lead to a more empathetic, understanding, and compassionate society, where the worth of an individual is not measured by what they own but by their character and actions.

This vision of a society guided by principles of integrity, respect, and contentment may seem idealistic, but it is within reach. It starts with each of us, in our daily decisions and interactions, choosing to respect the boundaries of others and finding contentment in what we have. By doing so, we contribute to building a society that reflects these values, where relationships are cherished, communities are strong, and individuals are valued for who they are, not what they possess.

At first glance, the commandments "Do not murder" and "Do not steal" appear clear-cut directives. However, when we delve into the teachings of Yeshua, we uncover a deeper, more profound layer to these instructions. Yeshua urges us to examine the conditions of our hearts, to recognise and confront the anger and greed that dwell within us. This introspective journey isn't just about adhering to the letter of the law; it's about embracing a transformation that could radically change the fabric of society.

Imagine a world where this approach is widespread. If we address the root causes of violence by tackling the anger that fuels it, we could witness a significant reduction in acts of aggression and harm.

But Yeshua's teachings push us further, encouraging a justice system prioritising restoration over mere punishment. Such a system would not only seek to rectify the wrongs done but also to heal the relationships and communities torn apart by those wrongs.

Furthermore, consider the impact on our economies if greed was no longer the driving force. Instead, economies grounded in fairness and generosity would emerge, where the focus shifts from accumulating wealth at the expense of others to ensuring that everyone has enough. This is not a utopian fantasy but a practical vision of what society would look like when we take Yeshua's teachings to heart.

A society that genuinely upholds the value of every life and respects both personal and communal property is within reach. Such a society would not only reduce instances of theft and violence but also cultivate an environment where peace and prosperity are not just for a privileged few but accessible to all.

By looking beyond the surface of these commandments and applying them in the expansive way Yeshua taught, we could pave the way for an era of unprecedented peace and prosperity. This transformative shift would redefine our relationships with one another and the world around us, creating a legacy of compassion, justice, and generosity for generations to come.

The very bedrock of humility is built upon a deep-seated reverence for the Divine; a principle echoed through the ages in the first and foremost commandments. These commandments, which instruct us to honour no gods before the Almighty and to refrain from taking the Lord's name in vain, are not merely directives for religious observance but are foundational guidelines meant to shape our interaction with the world and the Divine.

Yeshua's earthly journey is a prime example of this reverence; his life was a testament to an unwavering respect for God. This profound reverence was not passive; it actively manifested in Yeshua's compassionate dealings with those around him. He demonstrated that true adoration of the Divine extends beyond personal piety, including acts of kindness, empathy, and understanding towards our fellow beings.

Imagine if society were to imbibe and live out these commandments in their true spirit. We would cultivate a society steeped in humility and driven by a sense of purpose that acknowledges our tiny yet significant place in the vast tapestry of existence.

Such a societal shift has the potential to counteract the pervasive culture of consumerism and narcissism that characterises much of modern life. Instead of valuing material possessions and self-aggrandisement, a community inspired by these principles prioritises collective well-being, empathetic engagement, and a dedication to fulfilling a purpose transcending individual ambition.

This isn't merely a theoretical ideal. By reorienting our lives around these values, we can foster a community where individuals are not merely self-serving entities but part of a greater, interconnected whole. It's about recognising that our actions, driven by a sincere reverence for the Divine, can ripple outward, influencing our society profoundly.

This approach encourages us to look beyond our immediate desires and to consider our legacy - how we impact our world and the lives of those around us. Embracing these commandments in their fullest expression could usher in an era of renewed social harmony, marked by a collective pursuit of higher, altruistic goals that celebrate our shared humanity and reverence for the Divine.

Visualise a world where the foundational ethos is deeply rooted in the Ten Commandments, as enlightened by Yeshua's teachings. Picture a world where the very fabric of our community is woven with threads of compassion, integrity, and respect.

It's a vision that might appear to be plucked from the realms of utopia. Yet, it beckons us with a powerful allure, urging us to ponder how these time-honoured principles could be the blueprint for our contemporary existence.

Let's entertain this thought: What if we, as individuals, choose to align our actions more closely with these teachings? Consider the ripple effect that such a shift in mindset could generate across our personal lives, neighbourhoods, and, ultimately, society. It's an introspective journey that invites us to question and, perhaps, redefine our values and priorities in a rapidly changing world.

How, then, could your daily life evolve if you embraced these principles more fully? Envision the depth of connections you might forge, grounded in genuine care and understanding rather than superficial interactions. Think about the trust and safety that could flourish within communities where everyone sincerely respects and looks out for one another.

This conversation is not just theoretical; it's a call to action. It challenges us to contemplate our role in nurturing a more compassionate, just, and respectful society. The path toward such a society is not a solitary endeavour - it's a collective journey that begins with individual commitments to embody these values in our daily lives.

Let us dare to dream of this compassionate society, but let's not stop at dreaming. Let's commit to tangible actions that embody kindness, honesty, and rest, cultivating an environment where these ideals can thrive. Whether through small acts of generosity, moments of truth, or taking time to reflect and recharge, every step we take is a stride toward releasing this dream.

As individuals we may not be able to change the whole world, but we can start to change our little bit of it. And if more individuals change their little bits of the world, collectively we can make a huge difference. In essence, the aspiration for a society steeped in the virtues taught by Yeshua is more than an idealistic fantasy; it's a feasible blueprint for a better world. And it all starts with our decisions, actions, and willingness to initiate conversations that matter.

Together, let's not only dare to dream but also dare to act, transforming that dream into a reality, one compassionate step at a time.

Chapter 16.

From Stone Tablets to Modern Hearts: Integrating the Commandments into Daily Life.

In concluding a book about the Ten Commandments and their impact on every aspect of our lives, it's essential to step back and consider the broader picture these ancient directives paint for us today.

The Ten Commandments, at their core, are not just a list of dos and don'ts handed down thousands of years ago; they are a foundational blueprint for building a life marked by integrity, respect, and a deep sense of community.

At first glance, these commandments may seem to be about restricting behaviour - telling us what not to do. However, upon closer examination, it becomes clear that they are really about freedom.

They guide us in avoiding the traps that can ensnare us in cycles of destructive no behaviour, whether that's through dishonesty, envy, or disrespecting the boundaries of others. By adhering to these principles, we are not limiting ourselves but rather opening up a world of possibilities for living a more fulfilling and harmonious life.

The relevance of the Ten Commandments transcends time and religion. Whether one is deeply religious, spiritual, or secular, the values they promote - honesty, respect, fidelity, and the sanctity of life and property - are universal. They encourage us to reflect on our actions and their impact on others, urging us to live not just for ourselves but as part of a larger community where everyone's well being is interconnected.

Incorporating the Ten Commandments into every aspect of our

lives means more than just following a set of rules; it's about cultivating a mindset that values empathy, respect, and integrity. In our personal lives, this could mean being truthful and faithful, honouring our parents and those who have guided us, and respecting the belongings and rights of others.

Professionally, it calls us to act ethically, compete fairly, and respect the contributions of our colleagues. In the digital realm, it urges us to use technology responsibly, respecting the dignity and privacy of others.

As we close this exploration of the Ten Commandments, it's worth considering how these ancient guidelines continue to offer profound wisdom for living well. They challenge us to consider not just the letter of the law but its spirit - to look beyond the surface and understand the deeper values they represent. In doing so, we find a compass for navigating the complexities of modern life, grounded in principles that foster a just, compassionate, and thriving world.

The Ten Commandments remind us that our choices and actions ripple outwards, affecting not just our lives but those around us. By striving to embody the values they espouse, we contribute to a society built on mutual respect, integrity, and a shared sense of humanity. In the end, these commandments offer not just rules for living but a vision for a better world - one that we can all work towards, one choice at a time.

Chapter 17.

In the Company of the Faithful: Accountability as a Pathway and Foundation for Godly Humility.

Living a life aligned with what God desires for us is a journey filled with challenges and rewards. This journey is not meant to be traveled alone; having someone to whom we are genuinely accountable plays a crucial role in ensuring we stay on the right path.

Accountability, in its essence, means having someone who knows our strengths and weaknesses, supports our goals, and helps us recognize when we deviate from them. It's about openness, trust, and a shared commitment to growth.

This chapter explores the critical role of accountability in aligning our lives with God's purpose, highlighting its importance in fostering true humility. By embracing true and genuine accountability, we can guard against such pitfalls as becoming controlling, arrogant, and self-seeking, ensuring that our actions reflect divine intentions.

At the core of many spiritual teachings is the concept of living a life beyond our own selfish desires. To live as God wants us to live is to embrace values such as love, compassion, humility, and service. These are not merely abstract ideals but practical guides that influence our decisions, actions, and interactions with others. However, embodying these values consistently is challenging, especially in a world that often rewards the opposite behaviours.

One of the primary challenges we face in our spiritual journey is the temptation to prioritise our own needs and desires above everything else. This is where the concept of accountability becomes invaluable. Having someone we are accountable to means we have a mirror reflecting our actions and intentions back to us. This mirror doesn't distort the truth to make us feel better or justify our mistakes. Instead, it offers a clear reflection of where we are in relation to where we aim to be, spiritually and morally.

Accountability partners serve several vital roles. First, they are our confidants. They are the people with whom we share our deepest aspirations and our most significant struggles. This level of intimacy and trust creates a safe space for vulnerability, where we can admit our faults without fear of judgement. In the context of living as God desires, this means having the humility to recognize when we've acted out of selfishness, pride, or control.

Second, accountability partners are our cheerleaders. They celebrate our successes and encourage us when we falter. This encouragement is not a mere pat on the back but a reminder of our potential to grow and live according to God's will. It's easy to become discouraged or lose sight of our spiritual goals amid life's challenges. Having someone to remind us of our capabilities and the importance of our journey can make all the difference.

Third, and perhaps most crucially, accountability partners are our guides. They offer wisdom and perspective when we're at a crossroads, unsure of how to proceed. They help us discern the path that aligns with our values and God's desires for us. This guidance is especially important when we're tempted to take the easier path that leads away from growth and transformation.

However, the role of an accountability partner is not to control or dictate our actions. The essence of accountability is empowerment, not enforcement. It's about helping us see the options before us and encouraging us to make choices that bring us closer to the person God wants us to be.

This distinction is vital because the journey towards spiritual growth is personal and unique to each individual. What works for one person may not work for another, and true accountability respects this individuality.

One of the most significant risks of living without accountability is the tendency to become controlling, arrogant, and self-seeking. The pursuit of power and status often reveals a deep-seated need for this recognition and control, overshadowing the humility and service that are central to spiritual growth.

These behaviours are antithetical to the values God teaches. Control is often a manifestation of fear and insecurity. When we try to control situations or people, we're essentially saying we don't trust God's plan for us.

Arrogance, on the other hand, stems from an inflated sense of self-importance. It blinds us to our interconnectedness with others and our need for God. Being self-seeking means we prioritise our desires over the well-being of others and our relationship with God.

Accountability counters these tendencies by reminding us of our vulnerabilities and our dependence on God and others. It challenges us to look beyond our desires and consider the impact of our actions on the world around us.

This outward focus is crucial for spiritual growth. It shifts our perspective from "What's in it for me?" to "How can I serve God and others?" This shift is transformative, leading to a life filled with purpose, meaning, and joy.

The process of becoming less controlling, arrogant, and self-seeking is not linear or easy. It involves constant and honest self-reflection, a willingness to change, and the humility to admit when we're wrong.

Accountability partners play a critical role in this process. They provide the feedback and encouragement we need to stay committed to our spiritual goals. They help us navigate the ups and downs of our journey, offering a steadying hand when we stumble and a celebratory hug when we succeed.

In practical terms, cultivating accountability requires effort and intentionality. It means seeking out individuals who share our values and are committed to their own spiritual growth. These relationships should be built on mutual respect, trust, and a shared desire to live according to God's will.

It also means being willing to be open and honest, even when it's uncomfortable. We must be prepared to give and receive feedback with grace, understanding that it's offered in the spirit of love and growth.

Living a life that reflects God's desires is a profound and fulfilling journey. It's a journey not meant to be travelled alone. Accountability is the thread that binds us to one another and to God. It keeps us grounded in our values, humble in our successes, and resilient in our failures.

By embracing accountability, we open ourselves to a life that is not only aligned with God's will but also rich in love, joy, and purpose. This is the essence of a life well-lived, a testament to the transformative power of living in community, guided by a commitment to grow closer to God and to each other.

In conclusion, genuine accountability is not merely helpful; it's essential for living a life that aligns with God's desires. It keeps us humble, focused on others, and open to growth. This form of accountability challenges us to live with integrity, to serve with compassion, and to love without conditions.

It's a journey that requires courage, honesty, and a willingness to be vulnerable. But it's also a journey filled with profound rewards - deeper connections, personal transformation, and a closer relationship with God.

As we embrace this journey, let us remember the power of genuine accountability in shaping a life that's not only fulfilling for ourselves but also honouring to God and beneficial to those around us.

Chapter 18.

Yeshua's Teachings: A self-reflection.

This special questionnaire is just for you. It is not to make you feel guilty or remorseful but to light your path as you look closer into personal reflection and growth.

Think of it as a gentle friend guiding you on an exciting journey of self-discovery. It's all about peering into your heart and mind and seeing how your everyday choices, thoughts, and actions align with Yeshua's teachings.

Imagine weaving the ancient wisdom of the Ten Commandments into the fabric of your modern life. This journey gives you a precious chance to re-examine your life choices and moral direction. As you ponder these questions, you're encouraged to explore how your personal behaviours mesh with or clash with the values Yeshua lived by.

This exploration is filled with moments of quiet reflection and meaningful insights. It invites you to pause and think deeply about who you are, the ripple effect of your actions on yourself and others, and where you can nurture growth, kindness, and understanding in your life.

This isn't about judging yourself harshly; instead, it's a chance to grow in self-awareness and take responsibility for your actions. Ask yourself: How closely do my actions reflect the virtues of love, compassion, honesty, and humility that Yeshua championed?

The answers you arrive at are between you and the Lord. They don't have to be shared with anyone else if you choose not to, though having a like minded friend to be accountable to could help in focusing your thoughts.

Or you could choose to work through this process together with a friend who is on the same journey, helping, sharing and being accountable to each other.

Therefore, to get the maximum benefit, be completely honest with yourself, no matter how uncomfortable it may make you feel.

Then pray and ask the Lord to help you improve in any areas that concern or worry you or those areas where you know you could improve on or need help with.

Use the space provided after each set of questions to make any notes that may help remind you of your thoughts and concerns, and to stay focussed.

This is what makes the questionnaire so powerful for personal transformation. It encourages people to live in a way that respects the Ten Commandments and also breathes the spirit of love and compassion that is at their heart.

By embracing this journey, you'll find the strength to face your weaknesses, the clarity to appreciate your strengths, and the inspiration to live in a way that truly echoes kindness, integrity, and love.

The questionnaire is all about inspiring you to live authentically and with purpose, honour Yeshua's teachings, and help make the world a better place.

1. No Other Gods Before Me
- Do I prioritise any person, activity, or possession above my relationship with God?

- Have I allowed my career, relationships, or hobbies to become more important than my faith?

- Do I spend more time on social media, entertainment, or other pursuits than I do in prayer, study, and meditation on God's Word?

- How do I seek validation, comfort, or hope from sources other than God?

Notes:

2. No Idols

- Are there objects, people, or desires in my life that I value more than God?

- Do I idolise any celebrities, influencers, or public figures? Do I allow their opinions to sway me more than spiritual truths?

- How do I react when something I highly value is taken away or threatened? Does it affect my peace and trust in God?

- Have I created a mental image of God that conforms to my preferences rather than seeking to understand Him as He reveals Himself in Scripture?

Notes:

3. Not Misuse the Name of the Lord

- Do I use God's name carelessly or in a way that does not show reverence?

- Have I sworn falsely by God's name or made promises in His name that I didn't keep?

- In what ways do I represent God through my words and actions? Do they align with His character?

- Do I invoke God's name to support my personal views or decisions without seeking His will?

Notes:

4. Remember the Sabbath Day to Keep it Holy

- Do I set aside regular time for rest, worship, and reflection on God's Word?
- Have I allowed work or other activities to encroach upon this day, neglecting its purpose?
- How do I honour this commandment in a way that reflects the principle of rest and dedication to God?
- How do I seek to make the Sabbath a delight and a blessing to myself and others?

Notes:

5. Honour Your Father and Mother

- Do I show respect and appreciation for my parents or those who have acted as parents in my life?

- Have I tried to maintain a healthy relationship with my parents, even when it's difficult?

- How do I speak about my parents to others? Is it with respect and kindness?

- In what practical ways do I support and care for my parents, especially as they age?

Notes:

6. You Shall Not Murder

- Do I harbour anger, resentment, or hatred in my heart towards anyone?

- How do I manage feelings of anger or frustration in a way that honours the sanctity of life?

- Have I considered the broader implications of this commandment, such as respecting life through my words and actions?

- Do I actively contribute to peace and reconciliation in my relationships and community?

Notes:

7. You Shall Not Commit Adultery

- Am I faithful to my spouse in thought, word, and deed?
- How do I guard my heart and mind against temptations that could lead to infidelity?
- How do I nurture and invest in my marriage or preparation for future relationships?
- Do I respect the boundaries of marriage, both my own and others, in my interactions and relationships?

Notes:

8. You Shall Not Steal

- Do I respect the property and rights of others, both in tangible and intangible ways?
- Have I ever taken something that wasn't mine, including digital content or intellectual property?
- How do I ensure fairness and integrity in my dealings with others?
- Do I practise generosity and stewardship with the resources God has given me?

Notes:

9. You Shall Not Bear False Witness

- Do I speak truthfully and accurately, avoiding lies, exaggeration, and deception?

- How do I ensure that my words do not harm others or damage their reputation?

- In what situations have I been tempted to lie or conceal the truth, and why?

- Do I stand up for truth and justice, even when it's inconvenient or comes at a personal cost?

Notes:

10. You Shall Not Covet

- Do I find myself envying others for their possessions, relationships, or achievements?

- How do I cultivate contentment and gratitude in my life?

- How do I seek fulfilment and satisfaction outside of material possessions and social status?

- Do I trust God's provision and timing, or do I constantly compare my journey to others?

Notes:

Closing Thoughts.

In closing this exploration of Yeshua's teachings on the Ten Commandments, we find ourselves at the confluence of ancient wisdom and contemporary living.

Yeshua, often addressing the heart behind the law, invites us into a relationship with these commandments that goes beyond mere observance to embodying their spirit in our daily lives. As he articulated,

"If you love me, keep my commandments" (John 14:15),

We are reminded that our adherence to these laws is not for legalism's sake but as an expression of love and devotion to God.

Furthermore, Yeshua's summation of the law into two commandments, to love God with all our heart, soul, and mind, and to love our neighbour as ourselves (Matthew 22:37-40) - encapsulates the essence of the Ten Commandments.

In doing so, He does not diminish their importance but rather elevates our understanding of them, guiding us to live out these commandments not only in letter but in spirit.

As we navigate the complexities of modern existence, let us hold fast to these timeless principles, allowing them to inform our actions and interactions. In the end, our commitment to keeping these commandments, inspired by Yeshua's teachings, becomes a beacon of light in a world yearning for truth and righteousness.

Thus, we are called to adhere to a set of rules, and to engage in a transformative journey that shapes our hearts, enriches our souls, and reflects the divine love that underpins the universe.

The Ten Commandments are not multiple-choice. They are a divinely inspired moral framework for living a life that honours God, respects our fellow human beings, shows love in action, and gives a path to a fulfilling and righteous life.

In keeping the Ten Commandments, we show our gratitude to God for His guidance and love, and for providing us with timeless principles for ethical behaviour.

They are a beacon guiding us to live a life that is more compassionate, just, and fulfilling, building a harmonious society and saying 'Yes' to a life of meaning, purpose, and peace.

Printed in Great Britain
by Amazon